from
# Twilight
to
# Breaking
# Dawn

# from Twilight to Breaking Dawn

RELIGIOUS THEMES in the *Twilight* SAGA

## SANDRA L. GRAVETT

**CHALICE**
PRESS
ST. LOUIS, MISSOURI

Cover art: iStockphoto
Cover and interior design: Elizabeth Wright

Visit Chalice Press on the World Wide Web at
www.chalicepress.com

10 9 8 7 6 5 4 3 2 1        10   11   12   13   14   15

EPUB: 978-08272-10486  EPDF: 978-08272-10493

**Library of Congress Cataloging-in-Publication Data**

Gravett, Sandra L.
    From Twilight to Breaking dawn : religious themes in the Twilight saga / by Sandie Gravett.
      p. cm.
    Includes bibliographical references.
ISBN 978-0-8272-1047-9
1. Meyer, Stephenie, 1973- Twilight saga series. 2. Meyer, Stephenie, 1973—Religion. 3. Christianity in literature. I. Title.

PS3613.E979Z66 2010
813'.6—dc22
                        2010008559

# Contents

# Preface

Getting the flu, especially in the summer, generally never ends up to be a cause for thanks. In my case, however, I took to bed in May 2009 with Stephenie Meyer's *Twilight* out of curiosity over the big fuss. I read it in one afternoon and continued on subsequent days of not feeling well with *New Moon*, *Eclipse*, and *Breaking Dawn*. Then I watched the movie version of *Twilight* and found the online version of *Midnight Sun*.

The ideas about how the books and films played on religious themes and used religious images kept coming. But the real prod to write about it came after talking to people about their reactions to the series. I guess I had been hiding under a rock, as I had not realized just how invested people were in this story. Everywhere I went I met somebody who loved these books and, for many of them, I met a daughter or a granddaughter who shared the passion.

When I presented my work about these books on the Appalachian State University campus in September 2009, I found students also strongly connected to this world. A number of dedicated Christians shared with me how they understood these books as stories of faith, love, and sacrifice in the best of their traditions. I could have written an entirely different volume based solely on how they read these novels.

I completed this manuscript just as *New Moon* arrived in theaters and got to add a little from my viewing of the film. Part of me would like to wait and see *Eclipse* next summer before going to print, but I know that the movies merely add a few touches, and I am working more with the content of the books.

It has been quite a fun but busy time writing this book. I have been encouraged and supported by many, but would like to thank my parents, sister, and Parker Williams, Lisa Lanier, and Les Gura in particular.

# Introduction

Stephenie Meyer's *Twilight* saga (*Twilight*, 10/2005; *New Moon*, 9/2006; *Eclipse*, 8/2007; *Breaking Dawn*, 8/2008) took the young adult fiction world by storm. With more than 95 million copies sold worldwide, Meyer topped the list of best sellers in 2008, occupying all four of the top spots for the first time ever. The first quarter of 2009 continued her run with one of every seven books sold belonging to this series. Additionally, *Twilight*, the first of four movies, came out in November 2008 and grossed over $384 million in worldwide box office and generated $151 million in DVD sales with over 8 million units sold in 2009. The second film, *New Moon*, premiered in November 2009 and broke the midnight box office records for Friday screenings at $26.3 million on the way to a record $72.7 million dollars in first-day ticket sales and the third largest opening weekend ever at $140.7 million. The story of a young woman, Bella Swan, and her love affair with the eternally seventeen-year old vampire Edward Cullen further prompted an entire cottage industry of products, Web sites, and parties, and even resulted in record sales of clothing items worn in the movie. The *Twilight* soundtrack sold 3.5 million copies, and *New Moon*, released early because of online leaks, debuted as the number one album.

These books introduce a variety of topics from young love, to abstinence, to the value of family and friends. But the author, a devout Mormon, also infuses her stories with religious themes and images. Although by no means dominant, or even particularly overt, Meyer's use of religion provides for some intriguing interpretive possibilities. Biblical figures such as Christ, Eve, and Mary function as prototypes for her characters. The relationship between free will and determinism, as well as the importance of moral agency, threads thematically through all four volumes. Images of the garden and the peaceable kingdom provide frames for her story. Love as an agent of change and a motivational impulse for self-sacrifice also receives significant emphasis.

This examination of the intersection of religious themes and images and the novels/movie begins with a short synopsis of each

1

narrative to situate the reader. It then proceeds in separate chapters to explore the two major characters, Edward and Bella, with a focus on Edward as a Christ-figure and the use of an Eve/Mary pattern for Bella. Subsequent chapters will explore Carlisle's family history and its relationship to his role as "father" and a God figure, the necessity of moral choice, Renesmee as a type of Christ child, the similarities of the final battle with the Volturi to John's Apocalypse, and the human, vampire, and shape-shifter communities forged in the model of the kingdom of God.

### The Story

Narrated by the central character, Bella Swan, *Twilight* tells the story of her move from Phoenix, Arizona, to the town of Forks, Washington, to live with Charlie, her father and the sheriff. At her new school, she encounters a mysterious and beautiful family, the Cullens, and feels a particular draw toward seventeen-year-old Edward. She puzzles over his intense reaction to her, and he gradually becomes her protector by saving her from a series of dangers, including being crushed by an out of control van and an attack by four men on a dark street. As their relationship develops, Bella discovers his true identity as a vampire. Despite the fact that his family feeds on the blood of animals as a matter of conscience, Edward struggles to rein in his desire to kill Bella, first out of fear of exposing his family as vampires and then because of his love for her.

The complications of love between a vampire and human play out in a variety of ways. Bella's fragility in the face of Edward's physical power generates her desire to be more like him in order to secure the possibility of a future together. This theme plays out most strongly as three vampires passing through the region—Laurent, Victoria, and James—threaten her life. In particular, James inflicts significant harm, including a bite that could be the start of her transformation. Edward saves Bella's human life first by stopping James from killing her and then by preventing the change from occurring; Edward's love for her allows him to suck the vampire venom from her blood even as such action threatens to snap his control over his nature. They end the novel together, happy, and at the school prom.

The second installment, *New Moon*, picks up with a happy Edward and Bella, but the complications of her humanity quickly force Edward into a decision to leave her, never to be seen again.

A despondent Bella falls into a deep depression, alleviated only by her best friend Jacob and by her ability to hear Edward's voice during times when she faces potentially mortal peril. When Edward believes her effort at cliff diving ends her life, he decides to end his existence the only way he knows how: a visit to Volterra, Italy, a city ruled by an assembly of vampires known as the Volturi. Serving as a ruling elite, they will kill him if he exposes what he is publically.

Bella saves him, but their relationship draws the attention of the Volturi, and they insist that she must be turned into a vampire. With the support of most of the Cullen family, she stands prepared to undertake such a transformation and thus to seal her relationship with Edward. She expresses a preference for him to perform the act, and he demands marriage as his condition. The novel concludes with their impasse on this issue.

The third book, *Eclipse*, focuses on Bella and Edward's developing relationship and struggle over her evolution into a vampire. Bella's best friend Jacob, a native Quileute, also serves as a significant complication. Not only does he present himself as a rival for Bella's affections, but in the second novel his status as a shape-shifter is revealed. Capable of changing into wolves, Jacob's tribe, as well as the Cullen family, exhibit a mutual contempt while observing a treaty outlining their respective territories. Jacob's efforts to steal Bella from Edward never stand a chance, but her demands to keep both men in her life as partner and best friend force the two antagonistic communities into cooperation. Thus, when the vampire Victoria seeks to avenge her mate James and raises an army of newborn vampires to attack Bella and the Cullens, the Cullens and the Quileutes work together to their mutual benefit.

The final novel, *Breaking Dawn*, alters the pattern of the other books with the narrative voice beginning with Bella before shifting to Jacob and then back to Bella again. The story opens at the marriage of Edward and Bella and the subsequent consummation of their relationship. Bella becomes pregnant on her honeymoon, and no one, including her father-in-law and doctor Carlisle, knows what will result from the coupling of a human and a vampire. Renesmee's birth almost kills Bella, but Edward miraculously manages to transform her into a vampire. The infant who emerges proves remarkable. Jacob, the wolf, "imprints" on the newborn and becomes her protector. Others, however, threaten her existence and force the Cullens to gather a group of vampire and wolf witnesses to challenge the authority of the Volturi to kill her. A great preparation for battle ensues, but the newly minted community prevails.

Meyer's story, supposedly completed with this final novel, came to a positive conclusion for the young lovers, and plans to make movies are in process. But the author started the tale again, this time in the voice of Edward, and tentatively titled it *Midnight Sun*. When a portion of the unpublished manuscript appeared on the Internet in 2008, Meyer initially expressed her unwillingness to continue with the project. She then posted 264 pages online on her Web site, and this version serves as an official copy of the *Twilight* story reworked. References to this document will also be included in this book where appropriate.

# 1

# Edward

## Introduction

The *Twilight* saga presents Edward, a young and compelling vampire, not only as Bella's love interest but also as her savior, particularly in the first book. He takes on many of the characteristics of a cinematic Christ-figure identified by Anton Karl Kozlovic in his work on such characters in film.[1] To most readers or viewers, vampires as Christ-figures might not seem an obvious connection. Much of the literature and film from the modern West depicts these "undead" blood predators as life-taking rather than life-giving and as *loci* of evil as opposed to exemplars of morality. Vampire legends, however, connect in tangible ways to Jewish and Christian claims about the properties of blood as the source of life. Moreover, just as Christ's blood offers believers access to immortality, so also vampires exercise the possibility of eternal life through their ability to ingest blood.

This consideration of Edward will begin by exploring the associations between biblical ideas about blood and life, including an examination of how Christ's blood becomes a source for eternal existence. The relationship of these teachings to legends about vampires and particularly to the ways in which Meyer presents these legends follows. At this point, Kozlovic's listing of Christ-figure characteristics will serve as a guideline for thinking through how Edward corresponds to such conventions. Finally, two examples of Edward functioning in a Christ role outside of Kozlovic's paradigm will be articulated. A "transfiguration" occurs in both the novel and the film, but they do not correspond in detail. Further, Edward's presence even while absent in the novel *New Moon* will be likened to the function of the Holy Spirit in the Christian community.

### Blood and Life

The identification of blood as the source of life in Jewish and Christian religious teachings begins in the book of Genesis. When Cain murders his brother, Abel, the texts reports that the  blood of the dead man cries out to God from the ground (Gen. 4:10). Here the newly spilled liquid continues to contain the life force even apart from a body. The essential properties of blood become clearer in the story of the flood. There God commands Noah and his family:

> Only, you shall not eat flesh with its life, that is, its blood. For your own lifeblood I will surely require a reckoning: from every animal I will require it and from human beings, each one for the blood of another, I will require a reckoning for human life. (Gen. 9:4–5)

As the source of both animal and human animation, blood becomes sacred because the power of life belongs to the deity. God thus issues specific prohibitions, even to the point of death, for the one who sheds it (Gen. 9:6).

Such a ban likely stemmed culturally from an unwillingness either to assume or to violate the life of any other sentient being. If one crossed the boundaries designed to preserve the integrity of all bodies, one's own existence would potentially stand under threat. These taboos, then, functioned to maintain social and ethical boundaries and to promote community cohesion and cooperation. Further, in this context, God receives identification as the creator and sustainer of existence. Thus to ingest the unique qualities each being possessed violates the divinely created order by mingling varied life forms and attributes. Finally, to kill another encroaches upon the prerogative of God: only God gives life and, so it follows, only God can take it away.

As in Genesis, the more formalized dietary regulations of the people of Israel also forbid the consumption of blood: "for the life of the flesh is in the blood" (Lev. 17:11; see also Deut. 12:16, 23–24). The writers of Leviticus hold that blood does more than simply carry life; it also functions as a gift from the deity to atone for sin on the altar (Lev. 17:11). In this regard, when humans violate the laws of God and need to make amends, God requires a living sacrifice. Animal blood serves in the stead of the blood of the wrongdoer and makes an offering suitable to eradicate the offense.

Such thinking often confuses people in the modern West, who do not typically think of blood or life as an appropriate remedy for a variety of acts that violate community order. But sacrifice functions precisely to uphold rule in a time where police forces and an independent judicial system did not exist to determine a fair outcome in a dispute. Real as well as perceived acts against another individual or group could likely incite conflict between families, clans, or villages or even spur the onset of war. Instead of what contemporary people might think of as vigilante justice, sacrifice shed the required blood and channeled aggressive instincts of the person or community into a far less dangerous rite.

This idea of blood connected to life continues strongly in the Christian tradition. Ephesians 1:7–8a says of Christ "in him we have redemption through his blood, the forgiveness of our trespasses, according to the riches of his grace that he lavished on us." And Hebrews 9:12 holds that "he entered once for all into the Holy Place, not with the blood of goats and calves, but with his own blood, thus obtaining eternal redemption." In the same manner that animal blood provided a means to obviate violations of the law, the shedding by Christ of his blood on the cross becomes the essential component of reconciliation between God and the Christian community by removing the taint of sin. In this understanding, humans come into the world under the power of sin (the doctrine of original sin) and thus must die. Further, sin makes humans unworthy to dwell with God and prevents the possibility of relationship. On the cross, Christ serves as the sacrifice for sin by offering his blood in place of the blood of the guilty party. With the problem of sin solved, the blood of Christ further overcomes the power of death and opens up the possibility of life eternal with the deity for Christians who believe.

To signify their membership in this redeemed community, Christians engage in a ritual meal of eating bread and wine that symbolizes the ingestion of the body and the blood of Christ.For some Christians, the doctrine of transubstantiation holds that when a priest blesses the bread and wine, they become the actual flesh and blood of Christ. Of interest, this ritual led some observers of the earliest Christians to accuse the group of cannibalistic practices. Christian apologist Minucius Felix, for instance, writes of how opponents see the Christian Eucharist:

> Now the story about the initiation of young novices is as much to be detested as it is well known. An infant covered over with meal, that it may deceive the unwary, is placed before him who is to be stained with their rites: this infant is slain by the young pupil, who has been urged on as if to harmless blows on the surface of the meal, with dark and secret wounds. Thirstily—O horror! they lick up its blood; eagerly they divide its limbs. By this victim they are pledged together; with this consciousness of wickedness they are covenanted to mutual silence.[2]

Partaking of the blood of Christ, while emblematic of salvation to Christians, seemed an act of extraordinary barbarism to some outside of the faith. It more resembles the feeding frenzy of Laurent, James, and Victoria on a hapless victim in the *Twilight* movie or the imagined meal of the Volturi in *New Moon*.[3]

Vampires, who feed on blood in order to retain their immortality, thus share something important with the religious traditions of Judaism and Christianity. In the Meyer novels, blood also possesses great power. Vampire bodies function to acquire it; they have increased powers of smell, remarkable speed, and abnormal strength to aid in their quest.[4] But feeding on human blood does not, connect to immortality, as in Christian tradition. In the novels, a vampire "venom" that usually incapacitates a victim represents the key to the transformation from mortality to eternal existence. Not feeding makes vampires weak, but does not kill them. So whereas Christians seek a remedy to a mortal life infested by sin and thus by death, finding an answer in the blood of Christ, the vampire already has immortality.

The connection between the ideas about blood in the novels and in the Jewish and Christian traditions actually comes in the respect the Cullen family demonstrates for the prohibitions against shedding blood. Atypical of vampires as a group, they follow Carlisle's lead and feed on animal blood instead of taking human life. Edward describes this choice to Bella as humans opting to eat a vegetarian diet; while they still crave human blood, they opt to make the necessary adjustments for moral and ethical reasons.[5] The Cullens meticulously avoid human blood because, in some way, they all miss their humanity and thus exhibit great respect for its possibilities.[6] Edward, for example, defines himself as a soulless monster, but by withstanding the most basic instinct of a vampire he offers some semblance of resistance toward what he sees as depravity.[7] As in the biblical account, humanity here represents something positive and promising. Created by God and declared "very good," (Gen. 1:31) humans contain the capacity to live transformed by love (Rom. 12:9–13). The Cullen family seeks to tap into this understanding of what it means to be human and not to live as the animated dead, but as best they can in the tradition of human goodness.

Other choices confirm this way of life. The "father" Carlisle, works as a doctor because he experienced something akin to a vocational calling to preserve human life.[8] While he did create his "family" to assuage his loneliness and construct some sense of a "normal" existence, he transforms Edward, Esme, Rosalie, and Emmett when all lay at the point of death.[9] Moreover, at least Carlisle hopes that salvation may follow from this course of action.[10] The son of a minister, he refuses to accept his fate as predetermined simply because an unfortunate series of circumstances led to his becoming a vampire. Such a tenacious clinging to belief in the face of all evidence to the contrary offers some likeness to the final judgment scene in the gospel of Matthew where a person's final fate rests on how they treated others (Mt. 25:31–46). Instead of being dependent on blood for salvation, as many Christians believe, the Cullens rest their hopes in resisting its allure.

In this regard, Edward emerges as the ultimate exemplar of the possibility of controlling his nature by falling in love with a human whose blood he desires. Feeding on Bella literally would sustain his life, but he demonstrates restraint and even respect for her as a living being and does not submit to his instincts. Such control serves in the novel as an example of elevation of the baser self because he shows the possibility of channeling his behavior into something appropriate for social interaction and thus extends the possibility of peaceful relationship between a vampire coven and the human community. Moreover, as a result of his actions, he becomes a source of new life as a father and thus generates a different kind of immortality for himself and for other vampires—a true family tree. Via self-sacrifice, he pioneers something unseen and unknown before, and thus serves, as seen below, as a kind of Christ figure.

### Signs of a Christ Figure

Anton Karl Kozlovic's work on film includes an extensive catalog of attributes seen in cinematic Christ figures. While his writing deals specifically with movies, most of the qualities apply equally to literary fictional characters. For many people the idea of a Christ figure means a character with traits that directly reflect the teachings and actions of Jesus as understood through the church. Thus Christ figures must theoretically be explicitly holy. But Kozlovic notes at the outset of his work that not all such exemplars of Christ occur in religious films; "secular films can engage in religious storytelling about biblical characters, ideas, and themes without appearing 'religious.'"[11] That is, in a culture shaped significantly by Jewish and Christian traditions both consciously and subconsciously, the basic patterns of these stories influence writers and filmmakers, communicating effectively to a broad audience. Christ figures, therefore, might include the criminal Luke in *Cool Hand Luke*, E.T. the space creature in the film of the same name, or Gandalf the wizard in *Lord of the Rings*.

Kozlovic identifies twenty-five characteristics as a starting point and includes a non-exhaustive list of possible variants. This accounting does not cover every option for how a Christ figure can manifest; rather, it names the more obvious and frequent traits and describes the range of ways different filmmakers express them. Thus many features will overlap, some will combine, and others will not appear at all. Similarly Kozlovic cautions against looking for all of the elements in any one film or character or from reading too much into a given presentation. But he agrees with critic Peter Malone, who says, "the [Christic] resemblance needs to be significant and substantial, otherwise it is trivial. It also needs to be understood from the text and texture of the work of art, be it classical or popular, and not read into the text with Christian presuppositions."[12]

The use of Christ imagery, further, does not require that the character understand him- or herself in such a way or that the audience should read that character as Christlike in every trait or action. Rather, it means that the associations made in a work of literature or film suggest some basis of comparison. In some cases the character in question may share values attributed to Jesus,[13] but in others, the character might act in ways quite distinct from what most observers would identify as consistent with ethics and morals associated with him.[14] When assessing Edward Cullen according to Kozlovic's standards, a substantial number of Jesus' qualities emerge. The discussion below maintains some of the traits as separate categories and combines others for the sake of coherence in their presentation in the books and movies.

Kozlovic begins with the idea that Christ figures typically are "tangible, visible and frequently colorful characters, albeit sometimes only partially exposed or mysteriously delayed in progressive revelation fashion."[15] In the *Twilight* saga, Edward certainly fits these criteria. As Bella narrates the story, her obsession with him makes him an obvious focal point of the action.[16] Moreover, his vampire nature initially remains a secret from the community in Forks and from Bella. While she manages to get him to admit his identity over the course of the first book, the unraveling of his nature happens in stages as she pieces together a series of clues from the changing color of his eyes to displays of incredible physical strength.[17] The extent of what being "vampire" entails also continues to be developed in all four novels. As Bella interacts with more vampires, she understands their characteristics, norms, and lifestyles.[18] Most significantly, she enables Edward to tap into abilities he did not even know he possessed, such as fathering a child. The revelation, then, functions not only to let Bella know about him, but also (as seen in numerous other examples) to demonstrate something new about vampires to themselves.

Under this category, Kozlovic notes with regard to Christ figures: "their life story is frequently coupled with an odd, unexpected or obscure birth, origin, arrival, or creation."[19] Edward, like all vampires, was not born via the biological process of procreation. Rather, in the *Twilight* saga, an injection of vampire venom begins a process of metamorphosis that lasts several days. Alice, Edward's sister, offers one description and highlights the pain of a human body dying and a new vampire form coming forth.[20] Bella narrates readers through her own change in what *Breaking Dawn* presents as a fiery and excruciating procedure.[21] This strange birth ties loosely to another of Kozlovic's traits: "a decisive death and resurrection."[22] To become a vampire, human flesh dies and the person then begins life as a vampire in a transformed body.

The immortal body that results from this death and rebirth possesses both enormous capability and great beauty. For instance, Bella sees in this new form the entirety of the color spectrum and beyond, grains of wood and specks of dust. She also obtains an increased sense of taste and smell, as well as a strong sensitivity to sound and touch.[23] In describing her first glimpse of her changed self, she marvels at her perfection and strength.[24] This new and gloriously transformed body resembles what Paul envisions of the transformations awaiting Christians on the last day. In 1 Corinthians 15 he describes the new spiritual and immortal body as imperishable and raised in glory and power (vv. 42–44, 53; see also Phil. 3:21).

But Bella also observes some continuity with who she was before in something as small as the shape of her lips.[25] In this instance, her new body somewhat corresponds to the former and functions similarly to Jesus as described in the writer of Luke's resurrection accounts. Although the risen Christ walks with the disciples on the road to Emmaus in one story, they do not recognize him and must relate the story of the past few days. Only at the table, when Jesus blesses the bread with them (Lk. 24:13–35) do they know him. When he appears again, his followers see him as Jesus, but think they see a ghost instead of someone alive. Jesus says to them: "Look at my hands and my feet; see that it is I myself. Touch me and see; for a ghost does not have flesh and bones as you see that I have" (Lk. 24:39). Likewise, as Bella emerges transformed and virtually unrecognizable to herself, and also different to those persons who knew her, still something of the former physical self, as well as the former essence of the person, endures.[26]

Kozlovic further observes that Christ figures typically occupy a central role in a story and "are frequently crafted in either a savior mode or redeemer mode."[27] With regard to centrality, although Bella narrates most of the *Twilight* saga and thus becomes the character around whom all others move, Edward occupies a significant portion of the book because of his and Bella's love story and her obsession with him. Even in the second book, *New Moon*, where Edward's absence defines much of the narrative, he continues to appear regularly in her thoughts and to drive her behavior.[28]

Without doubt, Meyer casts Edward as a savior. *Twilight* introduces Bella as physically inept and often in mortal peril.[29] Edward consistently intervenes to save her from a number of dangers, including a van sliding on the ice and threatening to crush her against her truck[30] and a group of menacing men on a dark street.[31] Bella identifies Edward as her "perpetual savior"[32] and interrogates him about his level of interest in continuing to rescue her from an almost constant stream of misfortune.[33]

In Kozlovic's list, these saviors act willingly and "are frequently empowered to choose sacrifice out of their newfound knowledge, status, position, mission requirements, etc."[34] Initially the book shows Edward as unsure about why he acts on Bella's behalf. After he saves her from being crushed by the van, she questions him with regard to why he bothered since he treats her so badly, and he responds with his own confusion about his motivations.[35] But in *Midnight Sun* his sister Alice pushes him to recognize what prompts him when she tells him that she loves Bella, too, only to be met with his shock.[36] Although he still considers it a dangerous mistake to allow himself to be alone with Bella,[37] his love for her drives him to act in new and unanticipated ways. He goes so far as to express his willingness to leave her, no matter how painful, if it proves necessary to protect her.[38]

This willingness to sublimate his needs becomes a recurring theme in the books. In *Twilight* Edward confronts the tracker vampire James in order to rescue Bella. And when he discovers the bite that could change her, he controls his own instinct to drink her blood and instead sucks the venom from her bloodstream.[39] In *New Moon* Edward leaves Bella, claiming the relationship no longer works for him.[40] Only later does he explain that he concocted that story as a ruse to remove himself from her life to ensure her safety, and what great pain it caused him, to the point of attempting to get the Volturi to kill him.[41] This claimed propensity to put Bella's needs above his own also comes across in the third novel, *Eclipse*. In explaining to Bella his opposition to her becoming a vampire, he maintains that to turn her would prove him selfish; he wishes instead that he could become human for her.[42] With this type of selflessness, Edward demonstrates one of the central attributes of Christ as described by the writer of the hymn found in Philippians 2:5–11. The resolve required to give up status, place, and honor for another, the commitment to die for the sake of someone else, completely goes against the common assumption of what it means to possess the power of a god. Likewise, Edward denies his own nature in ways that confound Bella, his family, and the larger world of vampires.[43]

Kozlovic further claims that Christ figures frequently appear as outsiders within the communities where they live; "they are *in* the world but not *of* the world."[44] The entire Cullen family, as vampires, falls into this category according to the novel. They live in the town of Forks posing as parents (Carlisle and Esme) with five "foster children" (Edward, Rosalie, Emmett, Alice, and Jasper). The teenagers attend school there, but they all take lunch separately at their own table and do not appear friendly with other students or integrated into the social world of their peers.[45] To add to the image, they live in a house nestled far away from others residences, in the wilderness.[46] In a town known for its trucks and all-weather vehicles, they possess a garage full of top-of-the-line cars ( including a Volvo, a BMW M3,  a Mercedes, and an Aston Martin). These differences mark them as separate. Bella, new to town, observes their shared outsider status.[47]

This separateness relates to two other notable qualities. They all live double lives. Kozlovic argues, "Christ-figures usually have alter egos and/or double lives, and/or dual natures, one fantastic and the other mundane"[48]and "even if normal-looking, they are not quite normal."[49] Again, the Cullen family goes to great trouble to present themselves as ordinary. For example, Carlisle, the "father," works as a doctor in town.[50] But these seemingly "typical" human beings only go through the motions of an average human life. Each day the younger ones purchase food for lunch in the cafeteria that remains uneaten because they do not require it to live.[51] They do not sleep.[52] As for their appearance, while they resemble humans physically, they also transcend the normal in notable ways. Bella, for instance, notes their amazing beauty.[53]

With regard to appearance, Kozlovic also notes that movie Christ figures often have blue eyes. "Biblically speaking, blue is the symbolic colour of 'the heavenly origins of Christ (as the sky is blue.)'"[54] Symbolically speaking, blue is also "'the color of the divine, of truth, and of fidelity (in the sense of clinging to truth, as well as with reference to the fixed firmament of heaven)…blue is also a purity symbol.'"[55] While not blue, Edward's eyes do draw Bella's attention. When they first meet, she recalls his eyes as virtually black.[56] In their second interaction, however, she describes them as a more golden brown.[57] Later, when Edward asks her about a favorite gemstone, she replies topaz because of her fascination with the color of his eyes.[58] The tint here, apart from being striking both in the emphasis in the novel and in its expression on film, serves to indicate something vital about his character. The Cullens' eyes turn this color, as opposed to the typical red of a vampire, because of their diet.[59] In this case, then, Edward as a Christ figure does not come from heaven or express the divine. Rather, his golden eyes reflect a far more earthly orientation and thus reflect, in some ways, the longing for something beautiful in an earth-bound humanity. Hence, nothing of the blue sky appears here.

In this same category, Kozlovic contends that questions regarding normalcy frequently include questions about sexuality. "Christ-figures...are traditionally beyond the grip of debilitating carnality...the earthly missions of Christ-figures must always take overriding priority over their sexual desires."[60] In the case of Edward, he desperately wants a physical relationship with Bella, a yearning she shares, but he also wants to protect her.[61] In explaining the problem to her, Edward first talks about how the impulse to quench thirst takes precedence over all others for a vampire. He then continues to describe what kind of lethal force he could possibly unleash on her, even accidentally.[62] Even though Edward lacks a spiritual mission that forces him to put aside his bodily needs, his ability to control his sexuality, just as he resists his thirst for her blood, shows a mastery of the physical self typical of Christ figures.

The relationship between Edward and Bella also corresponds to a part of the Jesus narrative Kozlovic identifies by observing "there is frequently a Mary Magdalene-figure floating around the Christ-figure, a sexually tagged woman who is related to him in some close way, but who does not know how to properly express her sexuality with him."[63] Although the biblical story never identifies Mary Magdalene as a prostitute or as interested in a sexual or romantic relationship with Jesus, this perception persists commonly in many Western traditions. Most likely it initiated in the conflation of stories at the close of Luke 7 about an unnamed woman prostitute with stories that include the mention of Mary Magdalene at the start of Luke 8. This confusion became a part of official church teaching in a sermon from Pope Gregory the great in 591 and gets picked up in many modern treatments of the Christ story from *The Last Temptation of Christ* to *Jesus Christ Superstar* to *The Passion of the Christ*.

As virgins, both Bella and Edward lack sexual experience, and this certainly contributes to the awkwardness of physical expression between them. But Bella comes across as the more sexually aggressive in their encounters because of her intense responses to their physical intimacy.[64] Edward's strictly maintained physical boundaries not only demonstrate his reluctance to cause her any harm (He sometimes even lashes out at Bella for putting the responsibility for keeping her safe onto him.[65]) but they also reflect his ideas about appropriate and inappropriate behaviors and a basic difference in values. He wants marriage as a precondition for changing her to a vampire and certainly before he will even consider a sexual relationship. While she tells him that she does not want to be the girl married at eighteen and that marriage carries no meaning for him as a sign of commitment, he explains that as a man born in 1901, his morals differ.[66] His dogged persistence on this point seems to reverse general cultural understandings about male and female roles.[67] But in the context of a relationship imagined in a Mary Magdalene/Jesus Christ paradigm, the reluctant male[68] and aggressive, impulse-driven female make far more sense.

According to Kozlovic's traits, "other iconic Jesus behaviors"[69] loosely categorized as miracles and signs, also indicate a Christ figure. In the case of Jesus, he heals, exorcises demons, and performs a variety of acts that generally function to make people whole by meeting their most basic needs.[70] While Edward does not mimic such behaviors precisely, he does, as seen previously, possess a number of gifts, such as speed and strength, that allow him to act positively on Bella's behalf. Jesus also performed signs that demonstrated his nature and revealed, at least in part, his true identity.[71] As discussed below, Edward's abilities lead Bella to identify him as a vampire.

### Transfiguration

Another feature in *Twilight* draws attention to Edward as a Christ figure, although not strictly in a category Kozlovic defines. The transfiguration of Christ, when he demonstrates to a select group of his disciples his true divine nature,[72] closely resembles Edward's disclosure of his vampire body to Bella in both the novel and the film. The novel follows a timing sequence more similar to the account in the gospels by removing the revelation of identity from the appearance of a transformed physical self. By contrast, the tight proximity in the movie of Bella's recognition of Edward's vampire nature to his sunlit appearance functions to heighten the drama.

When thinking about connections to the transfiguration, the reader needs to walk through how Meyer constructs the relationship between Bella and Edward and how she comes to know what he is for any biblical parallels to make sense. Bella serves as the narrator of the novel and the movie. With the narrator appearing on the scene as the new girl in town, readers learn about the characters as she encounters them. With Edward, she notes immediately his good looks, but also a strange aversion/attraction dynamic he expresses toward her.[73] While much of their interaction mimics the wild mood swings of teenage relationships, a certain mystery surrounds Edward and his family, and Bella gradually observes various features that rouse her curiosity. Most significantly, he saves her life in an unusual and striking manner by getting to her side from across a parking lot and stopping, then lifting an out of control van threatening to crush her.[74] His refusal to acknowledge anything out of the ordinary happened, coupled with her previous fascination with him, pulls Bella in. She becomes focused on figuring out what makes him so different.[75]

Answers begin to come together on a trip to the Quileute reservation, where she runs into an old acquaintance, Jacob Black, with some others from his tribe. He tells her a legendary story of his people that identifies the Cullen family as "cold ones." This revelation sends her to do some research and to think through the things she remembers:

> I listed again in my head the things I'd observed myself: the impossible speed and strength, the eye color shifting from black to gold and back again, the inhuman beauty, the pale, frigid skin. And more—the small things that registered slowly—how they never seemed to eat, the disturbing grace with which they moved. And the way *he* sometimes spoke, with unfamiliar cadences and phrases that better fit the style of a turn-of-the-century novel than that of a twenty-first century classroom. He had skipped class the day we'd done blood typing. He hadn't said no to the beach trip till he heard where we were going. He seemed to know what everyone around him was thinking…except me. He had told me he was the villain, dangerous…[76]

At this stage, Bella slowly begins to see the reality of who Edward is, but struggles to understand what it means because she knows nothing like it in her experience.

The gospel accounts share a similar pattern in how the disciples come to know Jesus. For instance, they see him miraculously feeding large crowds (Mk. 6:30–44; 8:1–10). They witness him walking on the sea (Mk. 6:47–50). He heals the sick before them (Mk. 6:53–56; 7:31–37; 8:22–26). Further, although they hear Jesus teaching consistently, they fail to understand his lessons (Mk. 7:17–18; 8:14–21). Like Bella, the disciples feel a certain disconnect. While they know without a doubt what they see, categorizing their interactions with Jesus into something that makes rational sense proves too difficult.

According to the gospel of Mark, when Jesus and his disciples come to Caesarea Philippi, Jesus poses a question to his closest followers: "Who do people say that I am?" (Mk. 8:27). Various responses from Elijah to John the Baptist or another prophet ensue (v. 28) In other words, they turn to the most probable answers within their world. The book shows Bella as similarly confused about Edward's attributes and ready to offer some improbable theories. For instance, she suggests the *Spiderman* solution of a radioactive bite,[77] given that only pop culture can offer any likely possibilities to satisfy what she encounters with Edward.

In the gospel, Jesus then asks a second question, "But who do you say that I am?" (Mk. 8:29) to which Peter replies, "You are the Messiah." (Mk. 8:30). While Peter offers the correct answer and thus seems to get it, once Jesus begins to talk about what being the Son of Man means, things fall apart. Suffering, dying, and rising do not correspond to Peter's understanding of being the messiah. He must, therefore, protest. Jesus then offers a rebuke (Mk. 8:31–33). When the decisive moment comes for Bella to express what she knows about Edward, however, the narrative of the book presents her as reluctant. Unlike Peter, she feels reticent about making any dramatic or straightforward declarations. Instead, she tells Edward how Jacob related to her some of his tribal stories including vampire tales,[78] but she will not make the connection to Edward even when he asks if these stories bring him to mind.[79] When Edward continues to press her, she finally tells him that she dismisses any concern. For her, what he is matters less than her draw to him.[80] He meets her response with shock, anger, and mockery; he cannot believe she does not care. Somewhat like Peter in the gospels cannot grasp a suffering and dying messiah, Bella does not fully understand what it means that she is falling in love with a vampire.

By contrast, the movie does the revelatory scene quite differently. Here, Bella walks into the forest and Edward follows; they both seek resolution of this relationship after a series of interactions that pique Bella's curiosity and suspicion and lead her to investigate local legends and vampire lore. Once they stand alone and undisturbed, Bella speaks a set of observations about him: "You're impossibly fast and strong. Your skin is pale white and ice-cold. Your eyes change color. And sometimes you speak like you're from a different time. You never eat or drink anything. You don't go out in the sunlight." This catalog leads her to a conclusion," and eventually she tells him that she knows what he is. In turn he pushes her to declare her conclusions out loud. When she responds with a simple and clear "vampire," her declaration more closely resembles the direct response of Peter to Jesus' query. Similarly, this process of deduction rests solely on her experience of Edward, just as the gospel presents Peter as reliant on his observations of Jesus. While the legends of the local native people inform Bella, as Peter's knowledge of the traditions must have informed him, her response comes from seeing him, knowing him, and trusting her own response to him, much like Peter relies on what he sees, knows, and believes.

The gospel narrative continues in chapter 9 of Mark relating how, six days later, Jesus takes Peter, James, and John up on a mountain and reveals his divine nature to them. A transfiguration means to change form or to alter in such a way as to glorify. In this instance, as told by Mark, Jesus' clothing becomes dazzling white beyond any earthly possibilities (v. 3), and Elijah and Moses appear alongside him (v. 4). Lastly, a cloud appears and a voice speaks saying, "This is my son, the Beloved; listen to him!" (v. 7). According to the account, Jesus charges them to tell no one about their vision until after the resurrection, and the disciples struggle to comprehend what they saw and heard.

The film offers a scene that directly ties to this experience. Immediately following Bella's assertion, Edward takes her up a mountain so as to rise above the misty cloudbank that shrouds the forest. He tells her that he wants to show her what he looks like in the sunlight and reveal his true difference to her. Once they arrive, he steps into a shaft of light, opens his shirt, and turns to face her. The film shows him with a sparkling affect that Bella likens to diamonds. In the presence of such a transfigured body, Bella appears mesmerized and declares him beautiful even as he names himself a killer.

In the gospel of Mark, Jesus must explain to his disciples something of what they saw and what it means (Mk. 9:9–13). The way that the text presents it, Jesus talks about his death and resurrection over the course of several chapters in between curing those afflicted who come to him, teaching the crowds, and answering requests from the disciples (Mk. 9–10). But the disciples, while hearing him, simply fail to understand what he tells them and get concerned instead with their own needs. Likewise, Edward goes on to describe who he is to Bella. He demonstrates his predatory nature by showing her how all of his attractions lure his prey and then allowing her to see his speed and strength and to connect how they lead to his ability to hunt blood more effectively. Moreover, he confesses his past as a killer of humans as well as his immense desire to kill her, even though the family to which he belongs practices another way and feeds off the blood of animals. Rather than turn away frightened, she continues to express her trust in him and her confidence that he can maintain his control. Iin the film, she says that she fears only that he will leave and they cannot be together. And it is this scene where they confess their love to one another. Just as the disciples show themselves unable to put their interests aside and hear the message of Jesus, so also Bella lacks the ability to make a reasoned decision and steer clear of Edward.

The book takes longer to get to the big reveal. After their initial discussion about who Edward is, several days of more questions and answers unfold. Additionally, they must explain their newly forged connection to family and friends even as they attempt to learn more about their attraction and each other.[81] But several days later the two of them set out so he can show himself to her. In this instance, they do not climb any mountain; instead, they wander through the forest to a beautiful, magical meadow. When he steps into the sun, she reports him to appear dazzling.[82] Although he worries about provoking a reaction of fear, she remains calm and curious and wants only to stare at him and to explore his body with her hands. When he reacts to her presence, he must explain how who he is puts her in mortal danger made more acute by the depth of his desire for her. So she sees how his allure works with his speed and strength to make him what he is. But once he has shown himself to her and explained the profundity of his reaction to her, he can declare his love for her and she can express the same.[83] Once he has been transfigured before her, nothing stands between them to prevent an honest and true connection.

What stands out as interesting in the account given in the book, however, is Edward's response to Bella's acceptance of his vampire nature. He seems hesitant to step out and to let her see him in the meadow. Bella, having gone ahead of him into the meadow and the sun, must turn back and encourage him forward. When she, in turn, exhibits no fear or revulsion,[84] but instead moves in closer,[85] her response not only unnerves him but changes his perception of himself. Instead of seeing "the skin of a monster" as he says in the film, she affirms a dazzling beauty. Instead of moving away in fear, she offers a complete acceptance and trust in him not to bring any harm to her. Her admiration and her love evoke in him a latent humanity, as well as a primal maleness that confuses him.[86] The transfiguration in the novel, serves to inform Edward more about himself than to make any point to Bella. The acceptance she offers brings him to awareness of something within him he thought lost; he locates a suppressed but powerful sense of who he once was and, in some ways, still is. Now, instead of merely pretending to be human, but remaining aloof from any real contact with others, he learns that he can enter into a complicated relationship with a human for whom he feels love.

Jesus' transfiguration in the gospels, by contrast, points the storyline forward to the cross and resurrection. It is not a revelation for Jesus. It is simply an opportunity for Jesus' divine nature, unseen to the disciples in their ordinary experiences with him, to go on display. It both clarifies for the disciples what they had observed about Jesus and confuses them, as it offers a new definition of what messiah means. As with Bella, they cannot fully grasp what they now know. They do not comprehend what Jesus means about who he is, and Bella cannot understand with any complexity what living as a vampire means for Edward or for her as someone who loves him.

### A Continuing Presence

In the second novel, *New Moon*, Edward determines that he must leave Bella in order to keep her safe from all of the potential dangers he and his family present to her mortal life. In spite of her pleas for him to stay, he decides to make a clean break.[87] The harshness of his departure hits Bella like a death. She gets lost in the forest where this breakup happens, trips, and lies down, unable to move or respond.[88] The book further presents the loss as an ending for her by using chapter divides entitled October, November, December, and January with no content.[89]

The community that followed Jesus suffered through his death, but then experienced his resurrection. But a fear of abandonment haunts the narrative as Jesus prepares to ascend into heaven and leave his community behind. Thus he promises them a new kind of presence: the Holy Spirit, who will continue Christ's presence with them even in his absence. John 14:16–17 presents Jesus as saying, "And I will ask the Father, and he will give you another Advocate, to be with you forever. This is the Spirit of truth, whom the world cannot receive, because it neither sees him nor knows him. You know him, because he abides with you, and he will be in you." Dwelling within each believer rather than outside of them, this comforter will assist the community in recalling Jesus' words and actions (Jn. 14:26) and will convey his reality even though he no longer appears as physically present among them.

Likewise, Bella still experiences Edward's presence even in his absence. When she confronts or does anything that puts her in danger—menacing men,[90] riding a motorbike,[91] a hungry vampire,[92] cliff diving[93]—she hears Edward's voice warning her, begging her to stop, and guiding her.[94] Bella understands this evocation of Edward occurs only in her mind, but nonetheless feels something familiar in the way he speaks, and finds comfort in knowing he exists somewhere in the world.[95] As with the Holy Spirit, Edward's voice becomes an internal reminder of an external reality and a source of strength and hope.

According to the New Testament, the Holy Spirit dwells in all Christians, empowering them to live in peace (Rom. 8:5–6), to intercede for humans in their weaknesses (Rom. 8:26), and to tangibly demonstrate that they belong to Christ (Rom. 8:10–11). Bella's interaction with Edward during his absence functions similarly. She comes to understand that she needs to know Edward is out there somewhere.[96] This assurance offers Bella comfort and enables her to find the strength to live again, to pick up and keep going from day to day even without him tangibly present. The voice comes only when she does things that threaten to end her life and it serves to give her hope. Although she tries to experience his presence at the now empty Cullen home, she fails.[97] What she cannot grasp is that just as Edward served as her protector throughout *Twilight*, this continuation of his guardianship during times of distress makes sense. She knows him most fully in her moments of vulnerability. Finally, it occurs to Bella that Edward's vocal presence in times of trouble demonstrates his love for her.[98] While she prefers to be with him, she learns to trust in their connection and its power regardless.

## Conclusions

Many other possibilities for reading Edward, and for defining Christ figures in the *Twilight* saga. Jana Riess, for example, spoke in April 2009 to the ninth annual Mormon Studies conference and noted multiple connections between the books and Mormon teachings. Most specifically, she saw in Edward a storyline for overcoming the natural man and likened his relationship to Bella to Adam and Eve's choice to become mortal in order to have children and enjoy eternal relationships. She observed:

> What changes fundamentally for Edward is the new desire to live wholly for another…In "Twilight," Edward's self-control goes a long way toward throwing off the natural man. But it is Bella, working as a very clumsy Christ figure, who becomes a symbol of grace in Edward's transformation.[99]

And Edward consistently talks to Bella about how she awakened in him something new, something of his lost human self.[100]

Moreover, Bella does appear to be self-sacrificial. Her move to Forks comes to ensure her mother's happiness.[101] But most significantly, she shows a willingness to give her life to protect those persons she loves. At the outset of the book, and the movie, she speaks of how she never much considered her own death, but that dying for someone you loved might mark a good death.[102] This reference introduces the dramatic climax of the story where she goes off on her own to confront the vampire James. Motivated by a desire to assure the safety of her father Charlie,[103] her mother Renee,[104] and, of course, Edward,[105] Edward marvels at her resolve and at her willingness to sacrifice herself.[106]

While this reading offers some intriguing possibilities, *Twilight* still casts Edward more as the hero and savior than Bella, and Bella ends the book with her desire to be transformed into a vampire only temporarily delayed. For Bella, the eternal comes solely in this guise and the human must be transcended. Mortality bears down on her, and she sees clearly the eventuality of her own death.[107] To avoid this end, she expresses a definite willingness to leave behind family to follow Edward.[108] The typical teenaged existence simply holds no interest for her.[109]

As discussed in the succeeding chapters, Bella functions in *Twilight* in a way that mirrors the actions of Eve in the garden.

Then, as in the Christian story, receives her redemption as a woman through a recasting into a Mary figure in *Breaking Dawn*. In this long view, the true Christ figure of the saga becomes the child that she and Edward produce, Renesmee. A combination of the immortal and the human, Renesmee represents something not seen and understood before and manages to unite disparate communities into an amazing picture of cooperation and love.

Reading Edward as a Christ figure does not limit other possible interpretations or eliminate the persuasiveness of different readings. Nor does it seek to replicate in him the kind of perfection Bella as the narrator attributes to him. Rather, it casts him as a more complex and conflicted character, struggling with learning to love a creature far more fragile than he, and redefining how he understands himself and his nature in the process. In this sense, readers might think about issues such as what Jesus might have known about himself and his mission, how he experienced his power and his abilities over the course of his life, and what he felt about an impending death as issues central to his story, but only hinted at in the gospel accounts. As told in Meyer, however, the similarities that do emerge between Edward and Christ function more to bolster an idea of Edward as good, noble, and clearly designed to function as a savior to Bella both physically and emotionally.

## QUESTIONS TO CONSIDER

1. Seeing Edward as a Christ figure tempts many readers to make positive associations with him. What characteristics of Edward appear Christlike and promote a favorable assessment of him? What negative traits do you see that might hide behind Bella's fascination with him? Do these qualities make him function less like a Christ figure in the narrative?

2. Readers see Edward through Bella's eyes, and she, clearly, finds little fault in him. In *Midnight Sun*, however, readers get a glimpse of Edward's internal dialogue and a different perspective on the story. Does reading this new material change Edward's image?

3. The connections of blood to life are strong  in Jewish and Christian traditions as well as in vampire lore. Think about why blood serves as such an effective symbol of the life force and how blood connects meaningfully to ideas about atonement for sin and eternal life.

4. In a Christian understanding, Jesus willingly sacrifices himself for the salvation of humankind. The Meyer books want to present Edward as willing to deny himself for Bella. Do you agree that he demonstrates self-sacrifice? Or do you see him motivated, in any way, by self-interest? What about Bella? Is she self-sacrificial? Be certain to differentiate between being willing to sacrifice the self for others because it is the best and the right choice as opposed to meeting the needs of others because one does not see oneself as important otherwise (lack of self-esteem).

# 2

# Bella

## Introduction

Bella functions as the sole narrator for *Twilight, New Moon and Eclipse* and the primary narrator for *Breaking Dawn*. Because she is the character who relates the story, readers gain access to her thoughts, feelings, and perspectives on the events that unfold. Moreover, she offers a point of identification for the audience, being one of the few humans in all of the stories, a touchstone of normalcy in the midst of a rather fantastic cast of vampires and shape-shifters—at least until her transformation to a vampire in *Breaking Dawn*.

The ways in which Bella's character as a woman develops rest largely on a traditional Christian understanding of two biblical women and their relationship: Eve and Mary. One of the early church fathers, Irenaeus, expresses the connection of these two in his work, *Against Heresies:*

> For as Eve was seduced by the word of an angel to avoid God after she had disobeyed His Word, so Mary, by the word of an angel, had the glad tidings delivered to her that she might bear God, obeying His word. And whereas the former had disobeyed God, yet the latter was persuaded to obey God in order that the Virgin Mary might be the advocate of the virgin Eve. And as the human race was sentenced to death by means of a virgin, it is set aright by

means of a virgin. The balance is restored to equilibrium: a virgin's disobedience is saved by a virgin's obedience. For while the sin of the first man was emended by the correction of the Firstborn, the guile of the serpent was overcome by the guile of the dove [Mary], and we were set free from those chains by which we had been bound to death.[1]

In this paradigm Eve becomes the source of the fall of humankind because she ate the fruit of the tree of knowledge of good and evil and shared it with her man, who was with her (Gen. 3:6). The writer of the letter of First Timothy claims "the woman was deceived and became a transgressor" (1 Tim. 2:14b), and the intertestamental document Sirach states the case directly: "From a woman sin had its beginning and because of her we all die"(Sir 25:24). But Mary offers all of humanity hope in her willing obedience to God. By functioning as the mother of God in giving birth to the Christ, she shatters the old female prototype and recasts the ideal of woman into a new format that affords women power when they humbly submit to God, to their husbands, and produce children.

Cultural appropriations of this pattern often get spoken of in the shorthand of whore/virgin. That is, women either appear as the seductive temptress ready to snare unsuspecting men with their wiles or they remain "good girls" unwilling to express any kind of a sexual nature or desire outside of the bonds of a male-controlled marriage. Once within the safe confines of such a relationship, these women gain their identity, as well as status within a community, through motherhood. Thus, becoming a mother stands as the fullest expression of female sexuality. Any alternative to such a path gets characterized by the term "whore."

Exploring Bella as both Eve and Mary provides a number of interesting insights into her actions over the course of the saga. *Twilight*, for example, weaves its narrative around the idea of the garden, temptation, knowledge, and the possibility of death. In this book, Bella assumes the role of a curious Eve, tempted by Edward to seek knowledge of his vampire nature. But she eventually emerges as a temptress as well, especially in *Eclipse*. As her relationship with Edward develops, her quest for knowledge takes on a decidedly sexual cast, and she becomes a different Eve: a woman using her desirability to lure a man to her will. She reaches not only for Edward here, but also an eternity with him as a vampire. His insistence on abstinence and control of her body and actions begins a change in her, a control of her sexuality that culminates with her pregnancy in *Breaking Dawn*. Here, as with Mary, the opportunity to produce a unique child generates an unswerving determination to become a mother, even at the expense of her own life. Her resolve yields not only a new creation, but also a new community of traditional enemies united behind a common cause. Further, Bella's immortality comes as a result of this birth: literally because of the physical demands on her limited human body and spiritually because of how being a mother transforms her internally.

## In the Garden

*Twilight* opens with a biblical quote:

> But of the tree of the knowledge of good and evil,
> Thou shalt not eat of it:
> for in the day that thou eatest thereof
> thou shalt surely die.
>
> *Genesis 2:17, KJV*

From the story of the garden of Eden, the reader gets immediately prompted to think about how Bella's experiences reflect this setting. The description Meyer presents of the environment begins to answer some of those questions.

Bella moves from her mother's home in Phoenix, Arizona, to her father's in Forks, Washington. She considers this action a form of self-exile as she makes the change to give her newly married mother the freedom to travel with a husband who plays minor league ball.[2] But the dramatic change shocks her system. She misses the sun and the warm of the Southwest as well as the big city environment.[3] Her new home feels cold, wet, strange, and overwhelmingly green.[4] The shift from desert to garden, from a place where life struggles to exist because of the lack of water to a place where rain falls almost every day, dislocates her. She finds herself surrounded by woods, clouds, and water, where nature prevails and the things of civilization seem far removed.

For readers of the biblical text, likening Forks to the idealized paradise of the garden of Eden might seem strange. The biblical writers imagined this location in times where subsistence living required arable land, plenty of water, and temperatures favorable for human habitation. Much of the territory associated with the people of the Bible came up lacking on these necessities. Raising crops often required backbreaking work with rocky soil in areas that received scant precipitation. No major river provided irrigation. On the edge of desert, the temperature variations could challenge humans who managed to live in sparse enclosures with no heating or ways to cool the air. So the image of Eden, a locale with rivers and trees and plenty of vegetation, seemed something close to perfection.

But for Bella, Forks feels, at least initially, far from any ideal. The remoteness and small size wear on her. Several examples demonstrate her frustration. She plans a trip to Seattle, telling her father she needs a better library and the chance to look at some clothes.[5] Likewise, a shopping excursion to Port Angeles gives her an emotional lift just by her crossing out of the town limits.[6] Even the people, having all grown up together for generations, feel static to Bella in this cut-off place.[7] An outsider, she cannot find ease or comfort with her new locale or its routines. Small town confines are underscored when, after a near-fainting episode in school, Edward tells Bella she better get home before her father finds out. She responds with confidence that Charlie, as the sheriff and because of the size of his jurisdiction, already knows. This demonstrates to her the lack of privacy and the seemingly "no secrets" nature of small town life.[8]

The weather reinforces her forsaken mood with the heavy fog every day conveying a sense of being trapped.[9] As opposed to the vast vistas of a desert life, the dense, green woods shrouded in cloud and mist surround Bella. School also feels confining as Bella discovers she has already read most of the novels being studied in her English class[10] and has completed the biology labs in Phoenix.[11] No new challenges present themselves to stretch her intellectually or creatively. Home does little to improve her situation as she falls into a predictable pattern with her father of cooking, eating, doing the dishes and then her homework.[12] Only Edward notices her unhappiness,[13] but that fact alone gives her the possibility of escape.

For most readers, understanding Eden as confining runs contrary to the concept of it as paradise. But like Forks, it could be seen as restricting. The man and the woman, as depicted, did not, indeed could not, know human life in all of its fullness. Their lives, at least by inference, consisted solely of tilling and keeping the garden and being with one another (Gen. 2:5, 24–25). The story further reports a deficiency in a particular kind of wisdom: the capacity to differentiate good from evil (Gen. 2:17). In other words, they could not view the world with any complexity because they lacked the ability for moral decision-making. This childlike innocence locked them into a way of being that never presented any challenge or potential for growth. In this sense, the garden functioned as a kind of gilded cage. Its simplicity and beauty seemed idyllic, but its limitations eventually chafed.

Much like the biblical garden provides a setting for extraordinary events such as serpents speaking (Gen. 3:1-5) and deities walking in the cool of the day (Gen. 3:8), the primal wilderness of Forks, shrouded in fog and gloom, serves as the perfect setting for the mysteries of its many occupants. Meyer's garden conjures up creatures that could not exist in places like Phoenix with its bright sun and the strong overlay of civilization. For example, when Bella begins to figure out the mystery of Edward, she retreats to the woods, to a place where unexpected secrets seem far more appropriate, to think.[14] The use of Quileute legend by Meyer also heightens the quality of a mythological world steeped in folklore that allows Bella and Meyer's readers to push beyond usual ways of thinking.[15]

But Bella does grow, in some respects, to appreciate her new home. When she begins to fall for Edward, she acknowledges the area's draw, even if common sense dictated the opposite.[16] The word Eden can be read to mean "abundance" or "plenty" and relates in this context images of lush vegetation and extraordinary beauty. Forks, too, could transform into a vision of perfection, even for Bella, given the right circumstances. For instance, the meadow where Bella sees Edward as a vampire for the first time in the sunlight shows her Forks as exquisite, light, and magical.[17] In love and with Edward, she finds something magnificent in nature. But without that love, even this location suffers. In *New Moon,* with Edward gone, Bella returns and finds it far less compelling.[18] Indeed, in the movie version, she sits in a browned, barren, and dead space. Paradise, then, for Bella does not revolve around location, but rather depends on being near the tree that tempts her: Edward.

## The Tempted

In the garden of Forks, Bella assumes the role of Eve. Several clues point the reader/viewer in this direction, including the use of the popular idea of an apple as the fruit on the tree of the knowledge of good and evil. For instance, when Bella first sees the

Cullen family at school, she watches Alice throw away her lunch, which includes an untouched soda and an apple.[19] Likewise in the movie, Edward approaches her in the cafeteria as she selects her meal. An apple on her tray begins to fall and he bounces it off of his foot and extends it to her in both hands as he speaks her name. That shot, of some interest, replicates the cover art of the novel, where two pale white hands cradle a perfect red apple.

In the biblical text, when the serpent comes to the human couple and calls attention to the fruit on the tree of the knowledge of good and evil, it questions them about God's command not to eat from that particular tree. Then it tells them, quite rightly, about its consumption: "You will not die; for God knows that when you eat of it your eyes will be opened, and you will be like God, knowing good and evil." (Gen. 3:4–5). The woman assesses the options before them and sees in this fruit something beautiful and beneficial and thus moves without hesitation to taste it (Gen. 3:6). In many Christian readings, this moment stands out as the fall of humanity into sin as they disobey God.[20] A series of punishments ensues (Gen. 3:14–19) and the couple gets banished from the garden (Gen. 3:23–24).

Other interpretations, however, recognize courage in her actions and view the couple as stepping away from an ideal into reality. As Susan Niditch indicates about the woman, "she is no easy prey for a seducing demon, as later tradition represents her, but a conscious actor choosing knowledge. Together with the snake, she is a bringer of culture."[21] While the decision to eat the fruit produces particular consequences, such as the necessity to struggle to produce food, difficulties with childbearing, and eventual death, these items do not punish the couple. They simply become aware of life's hardships. Just as children awaken from their innocence as they grow older and come to see the world with less naïveté, so also do the man and woman realize the complications in and fragility of their existence, and struggle with more complex moral and ethical dilemmas. Rather than a "fall" from grace, they enter into life as engaged and aware participants, cognizant of their own weaknesses and shortcomings. They obtain knowledge and with such comes both blessing and curse.

Bella, likewise, wants to know more. The movie suggests connections to the biblical narrative more clearly than the novel. For example, in the cafeteria scene when Edward proffers the apple, he tells Bella, "if you were smart, you'd stay away from me." Like the serpent in the garden reminds the couple of God's commandment not to eat (Gen. 3:1), Edward here attempts to warn Bella off. But the biblical presentation of the serpent also suggests that eating the fruit will produce a positive result (Gen. 3:4–5) for the couple in the same way that Edward gives Bella an intense look as he expresses a desire for them to formulate some kind of relationship, even if it might not be the wisest course of action. Just as Eve showed firm resolve to make a choice to eat the fruit and acquire knowledge, Bella demonstrates a dogged determination to gain access to Edward's secrets. As with her biblical prototype, she rejects the premise of death as an inevitable outcome.

If one thinks of the woman's taking the fruit as both positive and necessary for humanity, then the issue of why God prohibits its consumption arises. Lee Humphreys suggests some possibilities for God's commands against such a step in his reading of the text, and his reasoning here also makes for an interesting interpretation of Edward's actions in *Twilight*. Humphreys writes,

> Yahweh God does not appear to want any transformation of *ha'adam* that brings his earthlings any closer to the essence of what he himself is. Did he initially set his prohibition on this tree to avoid this possible human transformation? Is he protecting his rank and place? Is it in terms of *his* stake and *his* interests that eating from the Tree of the Knowledge of Good and Evil is to be disallowed or its results thwarted? These suspicions are not easily deterred.[22]

He contends that God seeks to remain removed from and somewhat inaccessible to the humans by keeping them away from any thoughts that would change their perspective on the world and on God. In the movie, Bella sees Edward acting much the same when she tells him: "I can see what you're trying to put off. But I can see that it's just to keep people away from you. It's a mask." Refusing to play his game, she forces him to admit that what he shows the world does not reflect his truth. Thus, like Eve, when she reaches to take, she lays her hands on what is not willingly offered.

The novel does not employ the apple in similar scenes, but it does offer some insight into Bella's state of mind and why she makes the decisions to push forward with a relationship with Edward in spite of his efforts to keep her at a distance. While she intuitively acknowledges that Edward represents some kind of danger, she feels beguiled. Nervous and yet mesmerized,[23] she rejects a prudent course of not associating with him even when she becomes aware of the possibility he is a vampire. Again, parallel to the biblical Eve, Bella does not show any hesitation in her choices or her actions. She describes herself as a person who struggles to make decisions, but as one who sticks with a course once determined. [24] Even as she acknowledges the potential consequences, including her own death, she never pulls back from her resolve, or perhaps from her foolhardy need, to be close to Edward.[25] To use the biblical analogy, the fruit, in this case Edward, looked far too desirable to her eyes. [26]

The central conflict of the remaining novels emerges here. Bella's quest for knowledge changes as she grows closer to Edward. After he reveals himself as a vampire, she possesses the truth she so persistently sought. She then makes a striking pronouncement in both the book and the movie: "About three things I was absolutely positive. First, Edward was a vampire. Second, there was part of him—and I didn't know how potent that part might be— that thirsted for my blood. And third, I was unconditionally and irrevocably in love with him."[27] That love motivates her to continue her questioning and to crave other kinds of knowledge. Two items in particular stand out. First, she asks him about vampire sexual habits and the options for them as a couple.[28] In spite of his continual warnings about his potential to harm her in any interaction, she pushes for more intense physical contact. She trusts completely in his resolution not to harm her.[29] Second, she seeks to know how to become a vampire[30] and expresses a wish to undergo that process of transformation.[31] Bella realizes the only avenue to an eternity with the one she loves, the sole way she can generate the reality she desires, means embracing death.[32] Again, like Eve (Gen. 3:3-5), not even the very real and almost constantly recurring possibility of dying deters her from her course.

Edward's adamant refusal to allow her to be changed fails to end her pursuit of a new life as a vampire. At the conclusion of *Twilight*, they agree to a temporary impasse on the issue, even though she lets him and the readers know she will not give up.[33] *New Moon, Eclipse,* and *Breaking Dawn* all continue to develop around the connection between sexual desire, marriage, and Bella's potential transformation.

When Bella arranges a plan with Carlisle to become her creator,[34] Edward acts to derail her by doing the only thing he can. He uses the knowledge that she wants him to effect the change[35] as a bargaining chip to retake his position of prominence as the one who controls her body and actions. Their negotiations on this point reveal Bella as a woman willing to use every option in her arsenal to achieve her end, while showing Edward as seeking a patriarchal dominance based on marriage. This interplay proves thoroughly consistent with the Eve/Mary dichotomy. Just as the traditional understanding of these biblical figures posits marriage as a form of patriarchal control to subdue female sexuality, so also does Edward work to "tame" a sexually wanton Bella.

## The Temptress

Genesis 3:6 simply states that the woman ate the fruit of a tree she found beautiful and thought might taste good and give her wisdom, and then shared it with the man. But for Western culture, the idea of Eve as a temptress appears far more commonplace. Laurie Sue Brockaway states the basic premise: "perhaps the first seduction took place the moment Eve and Adam bit into the apple in the garden of Eden. From the very start, one gets the sense that a man (even the first man) could not refuse the urging of a naked woman. 'Oh Adam…just one, tiny, teenie-weenie, little bite.'"[36] So Bruce Springsteen points out in his song *Pink Cadillac* that temptations have been present ever since "way back in the Bible."[37] Likewise, the television show *Desperate Housewives* opens with images of the tree and the apple, and many of its print ads show seductively posed women in a sea of apples.

Again, while the biblical text says nothing about her persuasive abilities, later commentators attributed to Eve's sexual allure a power over the man's decision. One of the most influential early Christian thinkers, "St. Augustine of Hippo…wrote the following about women in a letter to his friend Laetus: 'What is the difference if it be a wife or a mother, it is still Eve the temptress that we must beware of in any woman."[38] Moreover, as Augustine indicates, because Eve serves as a paradigm for all women, it follows that the entire sex shares her characteristics. Biblical critic Nehema Aschkenazy plainly states the issue in her work; Eve sets a precedent and as a result, "woman is seen primarily as a sexual being whose moral weakness is coupled with sexual power which she puts to evil use. Woman's sexuality is for her the weapon with which she gains mastery over man and eventually destroys him."[39]

Meyer also imagines Bella as Eve the temptress. At the simplest level, it begins with her efforts to flirt with Jacob Black in order to learn what the Quileute know about the Cullen family. Although Bella worries about her technique,[40] she bats her eyes, flatters him, leads him to think she finds him interesting, smiles, and "smolders."[41] Later, recalling her efforts to Edward, she admits both her ineptness and her achievement. Bella believes she lacks even the possibility of such wiles, but Edward corrects her and affirms her attractiveness to young men in her circle.[42]

On a more significant level, Bella draws the vampire in Edward to her without any effort or even with any awareness of her appeal. The scent of her blood almost drives him beyond control at their first meeting. In *Midnight Sun* he describes the violence of his reaction and Bella's ability to transform him into a monstrous animal.[43] He proceeds in that telling of the story to plan his attack on her and on any others in his way, including a classroom full of students. Knowing such an exposure as a vampire would equate to forfeiting the life he cultivated with his family living on animal blood and among humans, he places the blame not on his lack of resolve, but squarely on Bella.[44] Even though she does nothing to provoke him, she becomes the guilty party, the temptress, simply by walking in a room. This assigning of blame resembles the man's reaction to God's censure in the garden; he directs all responsibility to the woman who gave him the fruit and to God, who provided the woman (Gen. 3:12).

As the relationship between Bella and Edward progresses, she continues to demonstrate a strange kind of unconscious power over him. Even though the strength of her blood's hold on him threatens the Cullens' place in the community, Edward keeps pursuing her. The novels include an almost constant stream of statements from him about his struggle to stay away and his inability to remain apart from her.[45] Not only will he risk his life and hers to be with her, he also shows an inability to withstand her even with regard to small things. For example, after Bella learns of Edward's identity as a vampire, they come together in the school cafeteria, where she dares him to eat, proffering (again, in an Eve parallel), an apple.[46] His response seals the biblical comparison. He takes a bite—even though he does not function biologically like a human—and, as *Midnight Sun* explains, it will require him to throw up the remnants later.[47]

But the knowledge Bella seeks takes on a more sexual tone over time. Meyer presents her as a woman with increasingly carnal appetites curbed by a controlling Edward. These new impulses also point to her as in the image of Eve. In his discussion of the garden, John Anthony Phillips observes, "Eve's sexuality is of special concern in the Western tradition. The Fall is regarded (whether literally or metaphorically) as a sexual event. Eve is guilty of wishing to be in control of her own sexual life. Some very deep, partially unarticulated fears are behind the male insistence that she be denied the freedom to make her own decisions about her bodily life."[48] According to this line of thinking, when the woman seeks the fruit, she actually reaches for human sexuality and it represents the desire for bodily pleasure. This choice assumes significance because she can thus select the possibility of producing life or not, of continuing the male line or refusing to do so. To assert their authority over this process, men establish structures to manage female sexuality, including the ideal of the virgin and the submissive wife. Both categories limit women's sexual freedom by forbidding sexual expression outside of the bond of marriage, thus channeling it into a vehicle where men rule and sex functions to produce their children.

As described, Bella and Edward's physical relationship affects them both profoundly. He tells her that beyond his thirst for her blood, he feels other, disturbing kinds of hunger for her, and she expresses that she shares the same appetites.[49] But she consistently appears more eager and prepared to push the boundaries of this attraction. For example, in the movie, they share, at his initiation, a first kiss in her bedroom. Because he struggles for control of his other senses, he instructs her not to move. She complies, at least until the kiss starts and then she aggressively moves toward him, on top of him, and begins to run her hands through his hair. After a brief response, he pulls away dramatically with a definitive "stop" and then tells her that he possesses more strength than he thought. "Yeah, I wish I could say the same" she answers.

In this scene, her sexual need seems to be the one more untamed. This pattern persists in many subsequent encounters. Described from her perspective, they always seem to end with him applying the brakes. A few examples drive home the point:

> "His mouth lingered on mine, cold and smooth and gentle, until I wrapped my arms around his neck and threw myself into the kiss with a little too much enthusiasm. I could feel his lips curl upward as he let go of my face and reached back to unlock my grip on him."[50]

> "The trembling didn't help as I tried to hurry to undo the buttons before he stopped me.

His lips froze, and I could almost hear the click in his head as he put together my words and my actions.

He pushed me away at once, his face heavily disapproving."[51]

"He started to pull away—his automatic response whenever he decided things had gone too far …'Wait,' I said, gripping his shoulders and hugging myself close to him. I kicked one leg free and wrapped it around his waist."[52]

The vampire, the one with the supposedly voracious appetites and the one who claims no soul or moral center, looks positively puritanical next to Bella's uninhibited needs. Even as he claims his reluctance stems from a desire to protect her from the real possibility his strength unleashed might accidentally kill her,[53] his actions cast her as more wanton, less responsible, and unable to assert control over her baser self.

Edward's reticence, however, when examined, demonstrates fears about and for himself. Enticed by her in a way he struggles to resist, she makes him feel powerless with her appeal to his more corrupt vampire nature.[54] His deep longing to appear as something other than the monster he sees in himself drives him to equate sexual control with a higher, more noble human self.[55] Moreover, his choice also reveals insecurities about Bella and about himself. For instance, marriage for him seeks to eliminate other men as threats. He sees Bella as evoking strong reactions in friends and acquaintances such as Jacob, Mike, and Eric,[56] and fears that she might turn elsewhere when he cannot meet her needs because of their physical differences.[57] Jacob presses him on this issue by asserting that Edward worries that if he let Bella choose her mate, she would not prefer Edward. Edward acknowledges this concern.[58] Marriage, then, provides him a margin of safety. If he cannot satisfy Bella's needs, sexual and otherwise, he still possesses her and keeps her away from the other men, shape-shifter and fully human, who would readily take his place.

Additionally, Edward's insistence on marriage demonstrates his lack of trust in Bella's commitment to him. He uses her physical desire as a bargaining chip to ensure he attains his objective because he fears that Bella will turn to Carlisle or Alice to change her if he concedes to her sexual demands.[59] Not only does he appear to lack any understanding of her obsession with and loyalty to him, but he again seems concerned that he might not satisfy her sexually and she might leave the relationship. Securing a lasting tie between them, even if it requires him to use what he characterizes as raging human horrmones to manipulate it,[60] becomes his way of asserting his dominance and of easing his anxieties. Marriage, in this paradigm, channels an aggressive female sexuality into something managed by the man.

Edward also acts to protect his soul. While insisting that his desire for abstinence before marriage preserves a morality useful to Bella's case to make it into an afterlife if such exists, Bella realizes something altogether different drives him.[61] Edward, the self-defined monster, understands himself as pure only with regard to his virtue.[62] His unwillingness to step out and take the risk of an intimate relationship, when he takes so many other risks, reveals a far more hidden agenda. It implies something uncontrolled about her sexuality[63] and, in particular, a fear of the power she possesses to take something from him. Never mind that he has learned not to desire her blood and to tame his vampire nature, never mind that he holds and kisses her routinely, and never mind that his refusal to transform her to vampire continually places her in mortal danger. To give in to her sexual demand, to be shaped by something she desires, means to accede to her in the relationship while also forfeiting his last bastion of purity and thus the possibility of saving *his* soul.

Without a doubt Edward controls, or attempts to control, many of the couple's interactions. When he determines it best for her future, he simply leaves her in *New Moon*.[64] When he considers her best friend Jacob a threat, he refuses to allow her to see him, even going so far as to disable her car[65] and requiring her to stage an elaborate getaway to reach Jacob.[66] When she wants to fight with the others in the face of the onslaught of young vampires, he makes her stay away.[67] Bella notes that he continually manages to achieve what he wants in their interactions[68] and that he looks victorious when he finally gets her to try on the engagement ring.[69] The pattern of their interactions becomes that she will go after what she wants regardless of the consequences and thus frustrate him by staying in constant peril. Such an untamed nature echoes common cultural perceptions of Eve as a woman who "lacks the moral discipline and reasoning skills to keep from being victimized by her senses. She has no intellect to hold her passions in check. She is the less rational, the more sensual of the pair."[70] Likewise, Edward routinely pleads with Bella to be reasonable.[71]

The dichotomy between Eve and Mary as described in the Christian theological tradition plays out here.

> The Eve symbol is associated with disobedience of male authority, risk taking, sensuality, and moral ambiguity. These attitudes and behaviors (which women are warned to avoid) are constructed as evil. The Mary symbol is associated with subservience, compliance with male authority, virginity, and moral certitude. These characteristics constitute the core Western cultural categories of the good with regard to women.[72]

As the temptress, Bella draws Edward toward a moral abyss. She threatens to undo the mask of civility he has acquired in his life among humans, she puts his family at risk of exposure as vampires, and she makes him vulnerable through his fear of hurting or losing her. To temper his reactions, he seeks to impose boundaries that curb her behavior.

When he finally determines to give in, to make love to her and then begin her transformation, she refuses him. At this point, Bella sees herself as causing pain to many people with her choice for Edward. Having realized her love for her best friend Jacob, she breaks his heart.[73] She hears her father's concerns that he will lose her.[74] She knows that she must show some responsibility toward her mother and to her new family as well.[75] So she chooses to acquiesce to marriage. Thus she begins to emerge as a Mary in her willingness to become a woman who puts the needs of others ahead of her own and assumes her place in a structure that presses her into choices she would not make on her own.

### Mary, Motherhood, and Eternity

If Bella as a temptress threatens Edward's control of himself, of the life he creates, and of Bella, she as a type of Mary annihilates any illusion of his power. A surface reading of Bella as she enters into wedded domesticity might initially indicate otherwise. After all, Edward finally takes possession of her as his wife and asserts his claim on her in a legal and binding way. Moreover, she seems to buy into such an appropriation.[76] As seen in the other novels, Bella gives up herself, her world, and ultimately even her life to secure Edward. What little that remained of her own desires—including to stay committed and yet unmarried—yields to his will and apparently becomes what she wants. Thus Bella as Eve, tied primarily to her attempts to seduce Edward, disappears, while Bella as Mary, functioning around marriage, family, and bodily transformation, emerges. This emphasis demonstrates how women characters frequently become coextensive with their physical selves and makes sense in the Eve/Mary framework given that "all four of the dogmatic Marian doctrines deal with sex and/or her body: the Immaculate Conception, virginity, divine motherhood, and the Assumption."[77]

But the change of Bella from one woman to another comes slowly as evidenced by the brief honeymoon of the human-vampire pair. At first, the question of sexual consummation of their union still drives Bella, as it represents her condition for agreeing to the marriage. Indeed, she continues to push the sexual boundaries right up until the night before the marriage.[78] But once she becomes a wife, she shows herself as the model of a timid virgin. Sitting on the bathroom floor at the outset of their honeymoon, she suffers a panic attack about going to him. The desire to take their physical relationship to the next level she expresses over the course of the novels disappears, at least briefly, in the context of the marriage. The text describes how she rejects all of the French lingerie her sister-in-law Alice packed. In this moment of truth, she cannot show herself as sexual, but chooses instead to wrap herself in a white towel. When she finally comes to Edward, she arrives in the color of purity and in a familiar object from any household.[79] As wife, she understands sexuality quite differently and appears virginal and domesticated.

At this point in the text, Bella articulates clearly the function of marriage as the proper conduit for sexual expression. Throughout the novels, Bella lacks confidence in herself as a woman desired. This deficit, at least in part, steams from understanding herself solely as an object of Edward's devotion and from fearing she cannot hold him in that position. Lacking any agency of her own or any power in the relationship, she repeatedly expresses her lack of anything worthwhile in the world apart from him.[80] Moreover, because he left her once, she retains the fear that he might do it again. For her, he remains too beautiful to fall for a clumsy, average girl, and his immortality rules out any kind of an authentic relationship with a human.[81] Only by giving up her life can she even hope to hold on to him, but as an immortal she will no longer possess the blood that functioned as the siren call to him. That allure, she believes, also involves the sexual chemistry between them. Marriage, then, provides her with the self-assurance required to consummate the relationship.

The initial marital encounter between Bella and Edward, while not described in any detail, nonetheless comes across as disturbing and illustrates the problems with any sexual relationship for this pair. While Bella awakens from the night happy and content, she discovers a number of significantly sized bruises.[82] While, at least according to Bella, this coupling of a delicate, virginal human girl with a more powerful partner leaves her physically satiated, she also emerges injured. A pained and remorseful Edward responds by once again refusing to sleep with her until she becomes a vampire.[83] Features of Mary begin to come into view here. The marks on her body demonstrate the appropriate womanly reluctance as well as Edward's power and control over the act itself. And he also determines whether or not to undertake such a course again. The telling of this story functions along the lines of a classic rape fantasy,[84] with Bella's battered body and complete lack of autonomy over the same serving as evidence. Although not coerced in any way, Bella gets the pleasure of the sexual encounter without having to appear to desire it, and thus she does not appear overly characterized by an aggressive sexual appetite. As Christine Seifert observes, "When it comes to a woman's virtue, sex, identity, or her existence itself, it's all in the man's hands."[85]

As mentioned previously, in much Christian thinking Mary, the self-declared servant or handmaid of the Lord (Lk. 1:38) forges a path for the redemption of Eve. Eve defies the command of God in the garden and, according to Christian teaching, brings sin and death into the paradise the first man and woman enjoyed. By contrast, Mary receives a somewhat perplexing visitation from the angel Gabriel, who announces that she will, as an unmarried woman, give birth to a child. In response to her queries, Gabriel tells her about the origins of this infant: "the Holy Spirit will come upon you, and the power of the Most High will overshadow you." (Lk. 1:35; note also Mt. 1:20 which says, "the child conceived in her is from the Holy Spirit.") While certainly not meant to be construed as an encounter that is painful to Mary, as with Bella's morning after bruises, the image of the divine power as a shadow coming over a passive and defenseless girl evokes some alarm. Neither verb (come upon or overshadow) indicates conception or activity related to it, but they do imply a certain amount of irresistible persuasion brought to bear and perhaps even a note of menace. Mary, however, embraces the new situation without hesitation and thus demonstrates her obedience and willingness to serve God.

The construction of Mary's willingness deserves some consideration; does she truly possess a choice? How would one refuse the divine? Does she put herself in jeopardy by a willingness to love God in this manner? But as scholar of Christianity Jaroslav Pelikan states it plainly: "It added to this definition of Mary as Handmaid that she was a woman and was therefore supposedly cast, by a deadly combination of nature and creation and fall, in the role of passive and submissive one, the vessel that received. Therefore she could be held up to women as a model of how they ought to behave, in submissive obedience to God, to their husbands, and to the clergy and hierarchy of the church."[86]

Both Mary's and Bella's sexuality falls under the control of a power outside of themselves. While Bella does manage to seduce Edward some days later and to enjoy a brief period of physical union with him,[87] Mary, at least according to some traditions, remains virginal throughout her life—a feminine ideal. Likewise, each woman's encounter with a being stronger and more powerful results in the same end: pregnancy. In Bella's case, no one apparently even considered the possibility.[88] Although some legends about vampires and humans mating existed, humans most often did not survive. Vampires, moreover, did not reproduce through sexual intercourse. Thus Bella's pregnancy shocks Edward and his family, and its unusual nature threatens Bella's life, leading Edward to want a termination.[89] Mary, similarly, carries the child of God from a conception outside of the norm. As a woman engaged, but not yet married, she would face community consternation and the assumption of either adultery or rape. Indeed, the biblical account in Matthew reports that Joseph, her betrothed, initially plans to sever their relationship (Mt. 1:19).

Ironically, however, pregnancy affords each woman a place from which she can function as more powerful and autonomous than at any previous point. The gospel stories present Mary as unquestioning in her acceptance of the pregnancy (Lk. 1:38), prepared to face divorce from Joseph (Mt. 1:18-25), capable of delivering the baby under difficult circumstances (Lk. 2:6–7), and ready to go wherever necessary to safeguard her infant son

(Mt. 2:13–14). In *Breaking Dawn*, Bella moves quickly from never having seriously considered motherhood, to being ready fiercely for it; the baby becomes instantaneously as important to her as Edward himself.[90] Edward, knowing that carrying such a strange child will likely hurt or kill Bella, wants to act to preserve her life.[91] But Bella immediately and decisively prevents him from such a course by soliciting the help of his sister Rosalie to function as her protector[92] and, by extension, her partner Emmett and mother-in-law Esme.[93] She further wills herself through a difficult pregnancy and a crisis delivery (with the physical assistance of Edward and Jacob).[94] Similarly, once she emerges as a mother, she demonstrates a continual willingness to put her child first, defending her from the potential danger she poses to her as a new vampire[95] and preparing to send her away if necessary.[96]

Each woman also emerges from the birth as a stronger and more capable in the eyes of admiring communities. Early in the Christian tradition, Mary received the label *theotokos* or the "bearer of God/ mother of God." As the mother of a divine being, Mary turned into no ordinary human being according to the teachings about her that began to spring up. She conceived through an Immaculate Conception, meaning it was free from the sin that haunts human existence. Similarly, her assumption into heaven meant that she did not suffer the same kind of death as the rest of humanity nor did she rot in a grave. Moreover, the doctrine of her perpetual virginity functioned to generate in her a spiritual purity. Most significantly, as Co-redemptrix and Mediatrix, she assumes spiritual duties as part of the divine plan for human salvation and relationship with God. All these features arise as the result of her carrying and giving birth to the Christ. Because Mary served as a vessel for the divine, the perception of the communities that knew her story found such reconceptualizations of her necessary to reflect the miraculous things she accomplished.[97]

Bella, similarly, changes dramatically as a result of the birth of Renesmee. Most obviously, she becomes a vampire and thus a being capable of eternal existence due to the near death caused by the delivery. Her old body dies and a new one emerges.[98] She also comes through the process not as the typically wild and vicious newborn vampire, but rather as a controlled being with an increased capacity for all the things she valued as a human.[99] Additionally, she possesses new and incredible powers, such as the ability to protect others from forces that threaten to destroy them.[100]

This last ability mimics one of the gifts of Mary seen most clearly in the Eastern Church. The Feast of the Veil or the Protection of the Mother of God commemorates a tenth-century threat to the city of Constantinople, where the veil of Mary remained as a relic. An apparition of her coming into the church with John the Baptist and John the Evangelist, among others, praying for the city, and then casting her veil over the congregation to protect them resulted in, according to the legends, the eventual relaxation of the threat. Such a tangible shielding of those persons who seek her assistance represents a more general characteristic of Mary as the Mother of God, as an intercessor for humans, and a protector of the Christian community. Bella's ability to serve in this role saves her family and the assembled friends from certain destruction. As a result, the vampires see her in a new light as indicated by their respectful admiration.[101]

## Conclusions

The power dynamic between Edward and Bella shifts dramatically as the result of her formation into a wife and a mother. As a newborn vampire, she now displays greater physical strength than her husband.[102] She also shows, contrary to other newborn vampires, the ability to manage herself and her instincts.[103] When she becomes a lover to Edward, she marvels at the intensity of the experience and appreciates their new equality.[104] Moreover, if possible, she becomes something different in his eyes as she produces his daughter and teaches him that he can value something more than he ever dreamed possible[105]

Nonetheless, her focus remains virtually the same. The intense emphasis on assuring the happiness of all others defines her. Bella's desires become subsumed in making certain the people she loves find security and satisfaction.[106] She continues, even as a vampire, much the same as she appeared in her human guise. But, as she herself concludes, no matter what her own individual power, she emerges as completely bound within Edward's thrall and is happier for that fact.[107] Indeed, her last act in the book comes in allowing him the one point of access to her marked off throughout the novels: the mind reader Edward could never hear Bella. She lets him in. No part of her remains separate or independent here.[108] As a figure of Mary, she models the perfectly domesticated woman under the control of the man. Although perfectly powerful in her own right and without a doubt capable of actions of import on her own, she willingly submits to a structure that subsumes her abilities for its own ends. Edward might worship her body and admire her abilities, but he also remains dominant over her.

## QUESTIONS TO CONSIDER

1. Readers of the biblical material can know nothing about the thoughts and feelings of Eve. Only her actions are recorded. This situation makes it easy for subsequent interpreters to assign blame to her for the problems faced by humankind. By contrast, Bella functions as the narrator of the text, and her motivations come across with some clarity to readers. Does knowing more about her help generate sympathy for her drive to understand Edward? Does it help elicit support for her desire to cut off her human life and become a vampire?

2. Bella appears to concede to Edward on major points in their relationship on an almost continual basis. He manages to control when and who will change her, for instance. He also determines the limits of their physical interactions. Does Bella ever come across as free and independent, or does she look controlled and subservient? Be able to point to specific instances to support your points.

3. The Christian story requires a new Adam (Christ) for salvation, given the sins of the first Adam in the garden. Likewise, the tradition poses a new Eve (Mary) for the weaknesses of the first Eve. Mary becomes a paradigm for all women in her humility, her willingness to give herself and her body for a higher calling, and her dedication and devotion to her family. Do you see any of these qualities in Bella? Does she in any way remake the typical idea of the "ideal" woman? If so, how?

4. If Forks is a type of garden image, what kind of a garden is it? The garden of Eden, according to tradition, looked like a paradise. Can Forks be understood as a paradise too? The garden of Eden also provided a place where people gained knowledge. Does Forks function in this way?

# 3

# Carlisle

## Introduction

"Father" to the Cullen family, Carlisle makes vampires of Edward, Esme, Rosalie, and Emmett in addition to serving as the exemplar for them and Alice and Jasper with regard to not drinking human blood. Although his story receives only scant attention in the four published books, readers get a more significant peek at his character in *Midnight Sun,* where he interacts extensively with Edward and presides regularly over family business.

Meyer's story line presents Carlisle as the son of an Anglican minister and vampire hunter from mid-seventeenth-century London. Although Carlisle did not and does not accept his father's severe and uncompromising faith,[1] he never questions the idea of God. Further, his belief in a universe governed by divine principle shapes the vampire he becomes. As Edward explains to Bella, when Carlisle realizes what happened to him in the change from human to vampire, he initially tries to destroy himself by jumping from high places, drowning, and starvation.[2] Faced with a lack of success because of the power of his immortal body, he discovers that drinking the blood of animals might serve as an appropriate substitute for human blood. Thus he learns to live not as a predator of humans, but rather in a manner that expresses love and compassion toward them.[3] He chooses to become a doctor and use his skills, even those talents unique to a vampire, to aid humans, and continues to hope for his own soul in the possibility of some kind of salvation.[4]

With regard to religion, as a creator and father Carlisle functions as a God figure in the novels. His ability to make vampires, his setting of the moral and ethical boundaries by which his family lives, and his place at the center of that unit all demonstrate these attributes. As with Christ figures, such a label in no way implies that a character exhibits such a self-understanding or pretensions to come across in such a manner. Rather, in analysis of how that character operates within a story, the comparison emerges.

### Creator

The biblical text never questions the existence of God. Presuming God's presence, it opens simply with God's creation of the world and everything in it. Two different stories mention the formation of humans. In the first, God expresses a desire to the heavenly beings to "make humankind in our image, according to our likeness" (Gen. 1:26). The resultant humans emerge simultaneously male and female and receive the instruction to continue in the process of generation via reproduction (Gen. 1:27–28). A second tale presents God as forming an *adam* or human from the dust of the ground and breathing life into it (Gen. 2:7). Subsequently, the deity determines that the *adam* would benefit from an appropriate companion and, after a series of efforts from the dust, constructs a woman from the rib of the *adam* as a partner (Gen. 2:18–23).

Carlisle also emerges in the *Twilight* saga as a creator by turning Edward, Esme, Rosalie, and Emmett into vampires. According to Meyer's mythology, the process of forming a vampire requires significant self-control. One must bite a victim to inject venom, but resist drinking their blood and killing them. When Alice details the procedure to Bella in the book, she likens the effects of human blood on a vampire to the pull of blood on a hungry shark; it taps into a natural instinct that proves almost impossible to resist.[5] Most of the family expresses doubt they possess the capacity to perform the task. When Bella asks Alice to change her immediately, she tells her she needs preparation to know how not to kill her.[6] Carlisle alone expresses no fear of losing his restraint in the course of performing the task based on his other successful experiences and on becoming accustomed to human blood as a doctor.[7]

When thinking about correlating Carlisle with the creator God in Genesis, readers must ask which creator. In the first story, God simply speaks and the creation happens (see Gen. 1:3, 6, 9, 11, 14, 20, 24, 26). The deity in this story functions as amazingly competent and in control. "The design of the world is not autonomous or accidental. It is based upon the will of God."[8] Everything happens in an orderly and untroubled manner. By contrast, in the second story, God seeks to make a companion for the *adam*, and a process of trial and error ensues. The animals and birds emerge, but no mate for the human (see Gen. 2:19–20). This divine figure seems more tentative, directly involved in the creative process, and willing to work slowly toward success. Carlisle comes across in Meyer's work as a kind of cross between the two. In his first efforts with Edward, he lacks certainty of success and does not do the process as well as he could.[9] Later, however, he gains skills and understands how to manage the conversion better and exudes more confidence. But he remains a scientist who learns through testing hypotheses, as evidenced in his work to understand Bella's pregnancy,[10] in his theories (which prove, by her narration, wrong) about easing the pain of her transformation.[11] He thus is more like the deity seen in the second creation story in Genesis.

But like God as a maker in the first creation story, Carlisle also constructs vampires in his image. When he describes to Bella his reaching the decision to change a dying Edward, his first such transformation, he says he saw in Edward's face something of what he desired if he could have a son.[12] This resemblance does not reflect a physical likeness to him, but rather expresses something about his character. What comprises this quality comes across most clearly in *Midnight Sun*. After Edward feels such a strong pull to Bella, he assesses his nature and his decision no longer to feed on humans. Meyer describes Edward as seeing himself with two faces: one a monster capable of inflicting great harm and the other a reflection of Carlisle's caring, nurture, and compassion.[13]

While theologians disagree on what it means for humans to be *imago Dei* or in the image of the divine, a similarity of traits in humans with those seen in the divine certainly represents the mainstream of interpretation. As David Brian Perrin indicates in his work, "*imago Dei* could refer to certain characteristics that human persons possess that resemble characteristics assigned to God. Rational thought and free will are frequently cited as two significant characteristics that reflect the *imago Dei* in personhood."[14] Similarly, person's embodying the image of God often are described as engaging in actions toward God designed to foster a relationship or as acting in a manner appropriate to promoting the values associated with God in the human community. According to Perrin, this stream of thinking about the *imago Dei* stands more in line with Luther and other Reformation thinkers. "From this perspective, the *imago Dei* is less about specific characteristics that humans possess and more about what people do, how they live out their lives together with God and with each other."[15]

This understanding also reveals itself in the *Twilight* saga. As presented, Carlisle's goodness evokes not only respect from his family, but also a certain reverence and a desire to emulate him. Edward, for instance, admires not only Carlisle's compassion but also his abilities to function as a doctor and work around blood.[16] He learns over the course of his time with Bella as a human that he, too, can exercise significant control of himself in that regard.[17] Thus a lifestyle choice revealed to him by his "father" opens up the possibility of a relationship Edward could not previously even imagine. Similarly, according to Alice, their adherence to Carlisle's ways makes the Cullens distinctive among vampires as they form a family dedicated to the security and well-being of one another.[18] Their bonds eventually extend to shape-shifters and other vampires; they move from a rather hostile treaty with the shape-shifters to full camaraderie[19] as well as to pulling together a community of vampire support to stand with them when under threat from the Volturi.[20]

In the biblical creation stories, readers never get any indication of a motivation for God's actions. What prompts the desire to form a world and to populate it with humans remains a mystery. According to the text, God does declare, in the first story, the various elements comprising each day's efforts as "good" (Gen. 1:4; 10; 12; 18; 21; 25) and the entirety as "very good" (Gen. 1:31). These assertions continue to puzzle theologians and interpreters as they determine what "good" means in this context. It might simply express orderliness and an affirmation that everything proceeds in a functionally appropriate manner. It could demonstrate that everything generated matched the intention of God. But outside of these rather ambiguous statements, nothing in the text discloses the mind of God with regard to purpose for acting.

In the second creation tale God states plainly "it is not good that the *adam* should be alone" (Gen. 2:18). This text portrays the deity as concerned for the emotional health of the created being and working to meet that need responsibly. But no overt clues appear about the rationale for why God began to create in the first place. By contrast, in the *Twilight* saga, Carlisle's choice to become a creator stems directly from a desire for company. Meyer asserts that most vampires live a rather solitary existence because their thirst for blood leads to a life focused on survival rather than the possibility of forming more significant bonds.[21] According to the story, after some 270 years alone and much exploration of both the human and vampire worlds,[22] Carlisle wants something he lacks. The wish for company and the ability to show and share himself as he is instead of assuming a human façade motivate his decision.[23]

But at least according to Rabbi Samuel bar Abba, Carlisle's motivation might possibly show similarity to his reading of Genesis. Numbers Rabba 13:6 says that "while the Holy One, Blessed be He, was alone in His world He yearned to dwell with His creatures." As with Carlisle, a need for authentic connection with something other than one's self drives God to create in this interpretation. Perhaps this avenue suggests itself because God recognizes the alone-ness of the *adam* and likely could not do so without some idea of what that state means. To show God's self fully and completely to the creation and receive, in return, the appropriate recognition from them of who the deity is certainly would link the God of Genesis and Carlisle as analogously constituted creators.

Unlike the impulse of God to generate something new and good, Carlisle struggles with this decision to make a companion.[24] For him, the benefits of intimacy with another vampire could not outweigh the loss of humanity that accompanied such a transformation. So when he finally takes the step, first with Edward, the decision rests in the pleas of Edward's mother to save her dying son.[25] Carlisle goes on to create his entire family in similar fashion. He transforms only persons already at the brink of death: Esme barely alive from jumping off of a cliff, Rosalie suffering from the effects of a violent gang rape, and Emmett losing his fight after a bear attack.[26] Moreover, he exhibits a similar motivation to that attributed to God in creating the woman for the *adam*: to form a fit partner. Esme becomes his mate and, at least initially, he changes Rosalie in hopes of making a companion for Edward.[27] While that pairing does not work out, Rosalie brings Emmett to him for just such a purpose, and Carlisle acts on her behalf to provide her someone to love.[28]

As a creator, then, Carlisle assumes the power to bring about new life in his image and likeness. The transformations, however, do not merely result in new vampires, but generate an entirely different kind of vampire community from anything known previously. Carlisle's image expresses itself most fully in character traits he passes down to his family and in the ways he chooses to live in the world. The extent to which he exerts influence becomes clear in the manner by which he instructs and leads his "family."

## God as Guide

When God offers the people of Israel a covenant at Mount Sinai, the biblical text reads: "Then Moses went up to God; the LORD called to him from the mountain, saying, 'Thus you shall say to the house of Jacob, and tell the Israelites: You have seen what I did to the Egyptians, and how I bore you on eagles' wings and brought you to myself. Now therefore, if you obey my voice and keep my covenant, you shall be my treasured possession out of all the peoples. Indeed, the whole earth is mine, but you shall be for me a priestly kingdom and a holy nation. These are the words that you shall speak to the Israelites'." (Ex. 19:3–6) As the one who freed them from oppression and performed remarkable feats to assure their existence, God informs the people of a desire to enter into a lasting and unique relationship with them. If they live as God directs, they will become something separate from other peoples and an example of the possibilities of dwelling in a divine light. If they choose to live in another way, they descend into depravity and darkness as they exist separate from the deity.

Edward Greenstein, in his work on biblical law, writes, "the story of Creation describes how God ordered the world by way of categories and infused his creation with life. Israel is commanded to safeguard those categories of God and revere life as the property of God."[29] In other words, God provides the law to humanity to preserve the creation as well as to structure the relationship between Israel and God and in the community of Israel itself. But to read God strictly as a deity that imposes rules and regulations misunderstands the biblical text. The Torah, meaning "story," or "instruction" or "teaching" does not merely lay out a set of legal requirements. Rather, it expresses a particular worldview, and then principles and goals emerge from it. "Broadly speaking, Torah is our way of life...It is the very essence of Jewish spirituality. It is synonymous with learning, wisdom, and love of God. Without it, life has neither meaning nor value."[30]

Carlisle not only has brought the Cullen family into existence, but like God in the book of Exodus, he also establishes a standard for his family to follow and a reason why they should undertake his rigorous lifestyle. In their practice of abstaining from human blood, for example, they attempt to retain some semblance of their human selves.[31] None of the Cullens sought out existence as a vampire, and this brings with it a certain burden. Carlisle cannot forfeit the compassion that marked him and suddenly live as a predator.[32] Rosalie cannot accomplish the one thing she wanted above all others—to become a mother—also a life-giving enterprise.[33] Even Jasper, a brilliant soldier, cannot ultimately endure the constancy of inflicting death.[34] They see in humanity a beauty and a potential that they crave for themselves, and they thus opt not to destroy that possibility in others.

Moreover, just as the people of Israel continually and consistently fall short of the behaviors God desires,[35] the Cullens have some missteps along the way. Emmett, for instance, twice kills people whose blood attraction for him proved too much to resist.[36] Rosalie avenges her rape by eliminating the men responsible, and she intimates Esme also suffered from the occasional lapse.[37] Jasper goes after Bella when she cuts her finger on birthday wrapping paper and he smells her blood.[38] Like God forgives the people of Israel,[39] Carlisle allows for such weakness as a by-product of vampire nature. But Carlilse himself remains pure[40] and keeps the expectation of living in such a way as a condition for belonging to their group. For him, the possibility of generating something unknown in their world proves worth the effort.

Carlisle's "law," like that of the God of Israel, proves aspirational. No one achieves it, outside of Carlisle, with absolute perfection. But the benefits of living as a family and sharing in such an enterprise transform them, and the law becomes something far more intrinsic to each of them. Just as Jeremiah 31:33 talks about how God writes the law on the hearts of the people, so also do the Cullens learn to do the things Carlisle asks of them naturally. His "law" forms them as a community bonded in love and makes possible for them as a group what previously might never have seemed attainable in the world of vampires.

### Father

A Christian audience immediately recognizes the connection between God and the idea of a father. But the link between this relationship and the biblical material might not be as readily apparent. The metaphor of God as a husband and a father receives strong emphasis in the Hebrew Bible and depends largely on the picture of the deity as head of a *bet av* (house of the father)—the basic social unit for the people of Israel. The image also serves to designate the place of God as ruler over the people of Israel as a nation. Such terminology for gods occurred throughout the ancient Near East "to identify them as providers and protectors. Biblical Israel followed this practice (Deut. 1:31; 8:5; Is. 43:6; Hos. 11:1), extending the metaphor to include the Lord's creation of Israel as his people (Ex. 4:22; Deut. 32:6; Is. 63:16; 64:7)."[41] The New Testament uses the term "father" 261 times with some 120 of those uses coming in the gospel of John. According to the texts, Jesus employs this language most often in moments of prayer (see, for instance, Mk. 14:36; Mt. 6:9; 11:25–26; Lk. 10:21; 11:2; 23:46; Jn. 11:41; 12:27–28; 17:1, 5, 11, 21, 24-25). The letters of Paul, by contrast, use it more as a title (see, for instance, Rom. 1:7; 1 Cor. 1:3; 8:6; Gal. 1:3) to designate the relationship of God to Christ or to the Christian community.

When considering the metaphor's meaning, the authority wielded by God provides a useful place to start. In terms of descriptors that reflect the structure of their social organization, the Cullens appear much like the *bet av* or "house of the father" in biblical Israel. For example, they come across as monadic or organized around one central figure. A good biblical paradigm here would be Abraham, who leaves his country, kin, and homeland to forge his own family unit (Gen. 12:1–3) after the death of his father. He serves to negotiate with other entities on behalf of his family (see, for instance, Gen. 12:16; 20:8–18; 21:22–34) and manages the affairs of his household (Gen. 13:8–9; 21:8–14; 24:1–4). Likewise, the essential place of Carlisle to the group he calls his own stands out as unmistakable to Bella, who cannot envision this family without him.[42] They exist as a unit only because of his efforts, and he manages and maintains them as an entity both publically and privately. To the larger community of Forks, he normalizes this group of vampires by functioning as the head of household (or the face of the family to the community) and holding down the job of a breadwinner like any other parent.[43] Although this young married couple with four teenaged foster children might appear somewhat odd on the surface, the cover story of a surgeon who cares for his own works because of Carlisle's ability to interact comfortably as a family man in a position of value to the town.

This rather traditional structure also earns the label patriarchal or centered around the authority of the male. Judah serves as a good biblical example in this regard. In Genesis 38, he arranges the marriages of his eldest son (Gen. 38:6) and orders the next son to follow the levirate law and impregnate her when his brother dies without an heir (Gen. 38:8). His decisions again become paramount when the younger son dies and he sends the widow Tamar home until his last son comes of age (Gen. 38:11). His authority in the family also extends outside of it. When he encounters, after the death of his wife, a prostitute he desires, he makes clear demands of her without any uncertainty (Gen. 38:16) or equivocation. Likewise, when his daughter-in-law turns up pregnant, he pronounces a death sentence no one questions (Gen. 38:24).

In *Midnight Sun,* a similar pattern becomes apparent. For instance, the Cullens convene in their dining room for a family conference. As described, Carlisle sits at the head of the table with his wife Esme by his side.[44] In a moment where decisions about the fate of the family will emerge, Carlisle assumes a physical position of power with the support of the "mother" figure Esme. Moreover, even as Rosalie and Jasper vehemently disagree, the pleas they want heard get directed toward Carlisle.[45] Similarly, Carlisle serves as the voice of the family in their interactions with other vampires. When Laurent, James, and Victoria appear in *Twilight,* he not only takes charge of the interaction and speaks on behalf of all of the Cullens but also makes clear his territory and demands respect for their home.[46] Additionally, when confronting the Volturi in *Breaking Dawn,* he steps out as the leader of his clan and represents their case before these officials.[47] Of greatest significance perhaps, in the family vote on whether to turn Bella, Carlisle emerges as the ultimate decision maker. Bella notes her intuition that his vote carries the real weight.[48]

The term patrilineal also applies. The biblical text places extensive emphasis on the family line. As any reader of the text knows, genealogical lists abound in Genesis (see Gen. 5; 25:1–4, 12–16; 36; 46:8–28 for examples). While wives receive occasional mention, the fathers assume the place of prominence for determining who belongs and how they fit. Similarly, the Cullen family traces its lineage around Carlisle and becomes his family in name as in practice. Edward, Esme, Emmett, and Alice all assume Cullen as their surname. Rosalie keeps her own, Hale, and Jasper adopts it as they pose as twins.[49] Although not clearly explained in the books, the best speculation for this bifurcation rests around the fact that Rosalie and Emmett function as a couple, as do Alice and Jasper.

Finally, in this instance, the family operates on a patrilocal pattern, meaning that the father decides where they live. In the biblical text, fathers shift families as necessary. Jacob, for example, determines to take his family from the house of his father-in-law Laban back to his father Isaac (Gen. 31:17–18) and then, many years later, moves his family to Egypt for relief from famine (Gen. 46:5–7). Meyer replicates that pattern. Given the cover story of the Cullens as parents with four teens, this practice makes sense. They move with the father's employment. For instance, when they depart from Forks in *New Moon*, the community members believe that they have gone to Los Angeles for Carlisle to take a position in a new hospital.[50]

In the New Testament, the image of God as father becomes a primary conceptualization of Christians for the relationship between God and humanity. Although the characteristics of a patriarchal head of household still apply, the emphasis switches somewhat to the nature of the connection between God and the believer. Marianne Meye Thompson cites four motifs central to the understanding of God as father revealed in the words of Jesus: "(1) the promise of God's provision for his children, (2) the concomitant call for those who are God's children to demonstrate impartial love and generous forgiveness of others, (3) the particular role of the Son in bringing or mediating the kingdom, and (4) petition to God as Father, especially, but not only, in times of need."[51] In looking at the character of Carlisle, all of these characteristics apply.

The New Testament text presents God as a father attentive to the needs of his children: the people of Israel. In the Sermon on the Mount, for instance, Jesus teaches that God will ensure his children get the appropriate food, drink, and clothing (Mt. 6:31–33). Likewise, Carlisle meets the financial, security, and emotional needs of his family. Edward clearly identifies Carlisle as the one who built the life the Cullens enjoy in Forks.[52] He provides the family with a home. In the books, the Cullens live in an old, restored house near the river,[53] while in the movie a modern glass and wood structure gives shelter to their family. In both, the isolation of the structure affords them both privacy and protection given their unusual lifestyle. Additionally, as noted above, Carlisle also wants to assure his children's happiness, and thus he turns Rosalie into a vampire with hopes of a match with Edward and then turns Emmett for her when she asks.[54] He also supports Edward in his fight for a relationship with Bella.[55] Further, he understands their individual needs, as with Rosalie securing justice for her rape[56] or Jasper's struggle to not desire human blood[57] and allows them to express themselves openly and without fear of censure.

Again, in the New Testament, God demands that persons in community demonstrate love and forgiveness toward one another. One of the clearest expressions of this command comes in Matthew 5:43–48 (see also Lk. 6:27–36) where Jesus teaches that one must not only convey love for one's neighbor, but also for one's enemies. Similarly in John 13, on his last night with his disciples, Jesus issues a new teaching to them to love one another (vv. 34–35). The ability to forgive comprises an essential component of love. In Matthew 6:14–15 (see also Lk. 6:37–38) Jesus' words definitely state that a person must forgive others in order to receive God's forgiveness. Probably most familiar, the story of the Prodigal Son in Luke 15:11–32 reveals the capacity of God to show mercy and love toward all "children" who desire such.

Meyer casts Carlisle as the God figure in the parable of the Prodigal Son to make a point about his capacity for and teachings about forgiveness. In describing his relationship with his father, Edward tells Bella about a period of rebellion when he sought out the opportunity to feed like all other vampires.[58] Although he only killed persons he terms as "evil," he nonetheless began to weary of the choices he made and what those decisions made him in his own eyes. He compares the welcome Carlisle and Esme offered to him when he returned home to that given to the prodigal son and speaks of how he did not merit their love.[59]

But Carlisle does more than show his children acceptance and love; he also demands that they exhibit the same in their interactions. With Bella's life on the line, Edward asks Esme and Rosalie to wear her clothes in an effort to mislead the tracking vampire James. In the movie version, Rosalie resists, but Carlisle says to her, "Bella is with Edward. She is part of this family now. And we protect our family." He will accept nothing less than her compliance. Likewise, in *Midnight Sun* when Edward wants to kill the man who attacked Bella, or at least wants him removed so as not to threaten other women, Carlisle assists him by arranging for an arrest so no blood gets shed.[60] Even when the family captures a newborn vampire in a time of conflict, Carlisle accepts the possibility of her surrender; a mercy that Jasper does not refute, but does not like,[61] and one that Jane, on behalf of the Volturi, does not accept.[62] In every encounter, Carlisle demands of the others in his family what he himself embodies.

In the gospels, Jesus comes to earth to inaugurate the promised kingdom (see Mk. 1:15). His work as the son of God fulfills what the father started with the people of Israel: building a community of people who dwell with God in peace and security (see, for example, Ex. 19:4–6; Deut. 7:7–13; Lk. 17:21; 22:28–30; Jn. 17:4ff). Edward, Carlisle's son, fulfills a similar role in *Breaking Dawn*. Carlisle wanted to live differently from other vampires and sought out cooperative relationships, as much as possible, with a created family: other vampires, the shape-shifters in the area, and humans. Edward's love story with Bella tested all of these bonds. His family needed to offer him support, even when they felt threatened by the potential outcomes of this relationship.[63] Edward needed to make peace with Bella's best friend, the shape-shifter Jacob, for her and for their child.[64] Other vampires needed to support his efforts to save his daughter.[65] Even Charlie, Bella's father, builds a connection with his grandchild—though he does not fully understand all the details of her life.[66] In loving Bella and in producing a child with her, Edward completes Carlisle's vision of the reality they could enjoy as vampires with a variety of groups. As discussed below, they create a true community bonded in love.

Finally, the New Testament presents God as father for the purpose of entreating divine favor both on a regular basis and in times of acute need. Nowhere does this aspect appear more obvious than in the Lord's Prayer, in which followers receive instructions to pray to God as a father (Mt. 6:9 and Lk. 11:2). In this regard, God appears as the one who can meet basic human needs and the one who inspires humans to live in a manner worthy of divine favor and in the divine presence. Carlisle, as seen previously, certainly inspires his family to something distinct from the vampire existence and provides for their needs. But he also functions as a source of wise counsel and support when necessary. Edward, for instance, turns to him when pondering how to handle the issue of the men who attacked Bella.[67] Carlisle also plays a significant role in the decision to turn Bella.[68] Moreover, he responds frequently and calmly to mitigate various medical crises.[69] In this regard, he functions as a steady presence that assures the continuity of his family and a calm, reliable center entrusted by all to do the right thing.

## Conclusions

To declare any literary creation as a God figure weighs down that figure with a challenging amount of baggage. Western readers frequently associate the idea of God with something wholly other and expect anything classed as deity to possess qualities such as omniscience, omnipotence, and omnipresence. But the comparison occurs on a far simpler level. The biblical writers constantly sought out ways to make the idea of God accessible to a human community. So even ideas such as creator and lawgiver found parallels in the human capacity to generate new life and to serve as moral exemplar. Further, the concept of father parallels a human role that carries great authority and power and yet also makes space for love, compassion, and nurture.

Carlisle, the vampire "father" of the Cullen family, functions in all these capacities in the *Twilight* saga. Without him, the family would not exist. Lacking him, they would not embody a way of being vampire apart from the norm. And absent his presence, they would prove unable to function as a unit designed to promote their mutual survival, their growth into their best possible selves, and their development of bonds of love and respect.

## QUESTIONS TO CONSIDER

1. Do you see Carlisle's upbringing as the son of a minister as an influence in the way he chooses to live his life?

2. How do you evaluate the choices he made in turning Edward, Esme, Rosalie, and Emmett? Is loneliness a sufficient reason to consign a person to such a fate? What responsibility as their creator does he bear for the decisions each of them make?

3. These individuals have functioned as a family for about seventy-five years. What do you think makes it possible for them to live together as they do? What do you foresee as the possibilities for their remaining together over the course of a possible eternity?

4. In the novel *Twilight*, Bella immediately notices a wooden cross (page 330) carved by Carlisle's father when she arrives at the Cullen home. In the movie, the art she observes is a collection of graduation caps from various locations where the family has lived. Why do you think the filmmaker chose to develop the story differently? Does it underplay the role of religion in shaping Carlisle and skirt Meyer's use of religious themes and images?

# 4

# Determinism and Moral Choice

## Introduction

Many people of faith ponder the question of whether humans possess the freedom to make real choices. The issue revolves around a couple of basic questions. If one believes that God, as a divine being, exercises control over the created order, then the ability of humans to act freely comes into question. David Basinger and Randall Basinger reduce the issue to its most simple form. "If we are really able to make meaningful moral decisions, then must we not be able to act against God's will? If this is so, then how can we maintain that all that occurs is in keeping with his will? If humans are free, how can God be sovereign? On the other hand, if God is in control, how can human choices be real?...Can we be free and yet predestined?"[1]

In the Meyer books, although God rarely receives mention, the importance of choice recurs consistently. The ability to steer one's own destiny stands out as a central theme in the series. Given Meyer's background as a Mormon, this emphasis seems reasonable. The Church of Jesus Christ of Latter Day Saints stresses the idea of moral agency as central to the belief system. Elder D. Todd Christofferson identifies its three elements: alternatives from which to choose and a law (from God) to define them; knowledge of the alternatives; the ability to make choices. He sees this last area as a gift of God.[2] LDS doctrine teaches that humans dwell with God prior to their lives on earth and must prove themselves worthy during their existence in this world of eternity with the divine. The choices humans make demonstrate capacity to live as spiritual beings in control of more carnal natures. It further allows humans power over their own destiny.

The *Twilight* books do not talk much about any larger cosmological order, much less how the humans, vampires, and shape-shifters found in Forks relate to any greater purpose. Carlisle, as the son of a minister, makes it clear to Bella that he believes in something outside of what they see and know—including a heaven, a hell, and the possibility of vampires having souls and the potential for an afterlife.[3] Likewise, Edward at least acknowledges the possibility of a creator and a place for vampires in the created order,[4] even as he imagines himself a monster[5] assigned eternal damnation.[6] In spite of such little material on the construction of the universe itself, the question about choice and whether or not humans, vampires, and shape-shifters have any moral agency frequently recurs in the books. While many of the characters want to see the world as determined, that is, each figure embodies a particular and unchanging destiny, all demonstrate openness to an uncertain and unknown future that often rests on the kinds of decisions they make. An exploration of these passages offers some insight into how Meyer constructs moral agency in her work.

### Teenaged Romance

In the dramatic, over the top way of young literary love, Edward and Bella each want to affirm that their bond as inevitable, fated, and thus the product of a determined universe. Edward indicates to Bella that in all his years as a vampire he sought something he could not define because she did not yet exist.[7] In this model of destiny, however, he credits his attraction to the unique scent of her blood and thus, the siren call it holds to one of his nature.[8] As a vampire, his physical design appears an overwhelming and untamable prompt to particular behaviors.[9] Killing emerges as something intrinsic to his bodily constitution and thus an inevitable part of who he is. Yet simultaneously he wants to hold open the possibility of making different choices. For instance, he tells Bella about wrestling between the morally right decision and his selfish desires with regard to his feelings for her.[10] But he believes nature will win out in the end, even if he resists killing her.[11]

Bella also conceives of her reaction to Edward in a rather fatalistic frame. When she first discovers he is a vampire, she considers her options, decides to be with him, and concludes no other choice ever truly existed.[12] Over the course of the stories, she continues to affirm this reality to herself and to others. She tells Edward repeatedly that his being a vampire matters not to her, even if it results in danger or death.[13] Moreover, she expresses her belief that their bond changed something in her and made their relationship unbreakable.[14] What motivates Bella, however, beyond the excesses of first love or perhaps the need for something stable in the midst of a rather erratic home life, remains unclear.[15] Her devotion to Edward defies logic in that she fails to recognize the real threat he poses toward her as the one who might kill her, the one who puts her in the path of other creatures who will destroy her, or the one who prompts her to sacrifice her life as a human. When he departs from her in *New Moon*, ostensibly to protect her,[16] she ceases to live any semblance of a normal life.[17] When Jacob offers her a viable alternative reality,[18] she rejects it. Once she meets Edward, she acts as if her life depends on being with him and that she cannot deviate from this fixed course.[19]

## Shape-shifter Determinism

The world Jacob inhabits also appears to him as quite fixed. In discussing his double existence, human and wolf, he tells Bella her he did not choose this life[20] and he cannot escape his fate.[21] Although recognizing his status as out of the ordinary, Jacob understands himself as thoroughly human, with a beating heart and vulnerable emotions.[22] He appears normal, although quite large, to the human eye.[23] He can interact with other humans, even if he must learn to control his temperament and power.[24] He can marry and father children.[25] Additionally, he shares this fate with his family and tribe. He distinguishes his uniqueness from that of Edward, who, at least to Jacob's mind, violates the created order as one made and not born.[26] He explains that his ability to change into a wolf comes about only because of vampires; the tribe performs these transformations only under threat.[27] So while the life Jacob leads appears routine on the surface, for him an unchangeable reality evolved over which he lacks any control.

Two features of pack life underscore the determined nature of the shape-shifter reality. First, they operate in such a manner that no one can defy the orders of the Alpha or leader.[28] Jacob finds himself bound like the others, at least initially, to Sam's commands. For example, he cannot tell Bella his story once Sam orders him not to do so.[29] And he and Seth, despite their misgivings, bow down to Sam's orders to kill the Cullens in the face of the threat from Bella's unborn child.[30] Only when Jacob assumes his birthright to claim a place as an Alpha male can he forge his own decisions and lead others.[31]

Second, many wolves "imprint" on their mates. This involuntary reaction[32] results in a powerful and unbreakable bond.[33] Although not necessarily a romantic or sexual link,[34] its effects demonstrate a similar power in that they last permanently. Not every shape-shifter experiences such a connection, but when they do, it illustrates a lack of autonomy over one's own fate and future. In seeking to understand why such a relationship develops, one might look no further than the close line drawn between human and animal in the shape-shifter world. The possibility that humans alone possess the ability to determine their destinies might be one of the most significant dividing lines between humans and the animals, and the shape-shifters exist on that dividing line.

### The Power of Choice

Mormons stress moral agency as one of the most essential human traits when it comes to salvation and relationship with the divine. In their understanding, following preexistence with God, humans receive a life on earth as a proving ground for their worthiness to dwell in the divine presence throughout eternity. In this earthly realm, God does not control human behavior, but rather allows people to make their own decisions and to choose their own way.[35] Mormon teaching includes the idea that Satan wanted to compel humanity to do good to secure the salvation of all, but God saw that this course would rob them of free agency.[36] For authentic choice to exist, people must have the option of choosing evil and separation from God.

In this teaching, Satan acted more out of self-interest than concern for humanity. He actually sought the praise and honor due to God alone. As a result of Satan's disagreement with the deity, Satan leads his followers to war against God in heaven. They lose. Mormons teach that Satan and his forces forfeit the capacity to embody as humans because of this defeat and thus cannot return and dwell in the divine realm. Given this state of affairs, they resort instead to tempting people to evil to keep humans from achieving what is no longer available to them, Satan's followers.[37] In other words, they prompt humans to make the wrong choices.

God, however, does not leave humanity solely to its own devices. Mormons recognize that God establishes laws and commandments[38] as a guide to proper behavior. Further, they understand that Jesus Christ comes to offer salvation from sin, but his actions do not remove the responsibility a person must assume for his or her behavior. At the most basic level, humans must progress toward the good of their own volition in order to make such choices true and worthwhile.

Even though Edward expresses a fundamental belief in a fixed universe, he continues to hold open the possibility of choice and appears to understand the power of such. For him, however, vampires lack the same potential to exercise real agency as humans do. Mormons teach: "genuine moral agency must entail necessary consequences."[39] In other words, one must choose actions fully cognizant of their repercussions and prepared to accept their outcomes.

The Cullens, by contrast, see becoming a vampire as tied directly to a loss of control over one's reality and possibilities. For instance, none of them enjoyed a natural end to their human life. Carlisle should have died in the streets of London;[40] Spanish influenza should have claimed Edward;[41] Esme's suicide should have been successful;[42] Rosalie should have passed away battered in the streets;[43] Emmett should have lost his fight with the grizzly;[44] and Jasper should have never been turned by a vicious woman looking for an effective head of her army.[45] Instead, they all experience days of great pain and then wake up to discover themselves trapped in an eternal existence dependent on a regular diet of blood. A residual sadness and/or anger often is expressed about these circumstances. Edward puts it all into a kind of shorthand for Bella by clearly stating that they all want to make peace with an existence about which they had no choice.[46]

That lack of freedom equates to significant loss. Rosalie, for instance, tells Bella that she does not like her because Bella wants to make a choice she never had.[47] To Rosalie,, Bella as a human can do something Rosalie desired more than anything: she can bear a child. In a permanently fixed and unchanging body, no potential for the growth of a new life exists.[48] Rosalie believes that Bella, at a mere eighteen years old, cannot know yet what she forfeits by not seizing this opportunity.[49] Similarly, Carlisle misses true companionship, but he wonders about the ethical implications of consigning another to his fate.[50] Even though he teaches his family a different way, being a vampire means combating a nature that always wants something else. He thus turns only a select few dying people in order to make for himself the life he wanted.

But perhaps most significantly, Edward thinks that becoming a vampire equals inevitable and eternal damnation.[51] He understands the power of choice for vampires with regard to some issues, such as whether or not to depend on human blood to survive, how to act toward other vampires and toward humans, or how to spend your time.[52] No vampire, however, can alter his or her ultimate destiny. As presented in the books, Edward believes he cannot recover his soul and thus can never hope for anything more or different than his eternal existence in the human realm or his own destruction and a permanent end, or, if it exists, an everlasting hell.[53]

Bella, by contrast, possesses the power as a human to make decisions of real import. Most consequentially, she can determine whether or not to become vampire.[54] But because she dismisses Edward's notions that he lacks a soul, she expresses no compunction about even the possibility of losing hers.[55] He cannot fathom, then, according to the books, her willingness to forfeit her life, to make an irrevocable choice that brings to an end the kind of reality he and his family value so highly.[56] Although only "seventeen" by appearances, Edward's many years of immortality give him a different perspective on the issue.

When you remove Bella's teenaged melodramatic expressions of and ideas about love from the equation, however, she does seem eventually to mature and to understand the consequences of her decisions. For example, the complications of leaving her family and friends to assume life as a vampire begin to weigh on her.[57] She also ponders the question of the constancy of love and if the possibility of a shift in her emotional state exists.[58] As her relationship with Jacob unfolds, she understands the possibilities and potentials in a new way. She sees that Jacob could have brought her much happiness, in another time and place.[59] Most important, when she gets pregnant—something made possible only by her humanity—she suddenly discovers something in herself she never knew before. She finds a deep and unwavering impulse to give birth.[60] As a result, she does everything in her limited human power to protect her child, including endangering her own life.[61]

While on the surface these decisions appear to show Bella growing up and becoming more thoughtful and considered in her decisions, ultimately she falls short on many levels. For example, she needs Jacob to push and manipulate her so that she can recognize her love for him and the consequences of choosing Edward.[62] More significantly, when she chooses to keep the baby, she understands it will most likely result in her death. The only possibility for her survival comes in a swift transformation into a vampire. But she abdicates responsibility for herself to Carlisle to ensure her survival.[63] She does not, however, ponder the (likely) possibility of severe complications or Carlisle's absence at their onset. She must struggle vainly against an encroaching death, and it comes down to Edward's extraordinary efforts to keep her alive by turning her.[64] In the end, Bella most often proves passive and generally cedes responsibility for major life issues and decisions to others.

Meyer's work presents both Jacob and Edward as better exemplars of the power of agency than the human Bella. Again, "Mormonism...shares with much of Christianity the view that the physical body introduces feelings and desires that may to lead one away from God. However, Mormonism holds that the key to rectifying this problem is not to mortify the body, but to employ moral agency and spiritual refinement to bring the spirit into mastery of the body."[65] As seen previously, Meyer presents Bella as a slave to her bodily desires in a manner that requires proper channeling. She might resent her humanity in terms of the limitations it causes her, but she also responds to Edward's kisses by losing any sense of her own will.[66] By contrast, Jacob and Edward each understand themselves as defined by natures tied directly to their bodies that they resent and want to resist. Each man sees himself as something of a monster and a potential danger to others.[67]

Jacob becomes a shape-shifter during *New Moon* and to maintain his human life, he needs to learn to have command over his literal animal nature.[68] To sustain a relationship with Bella, he must learn to control his hatred of vampires.[69] More significantly, if he ever wants to grow old, he must learn to manage the shifting.[70] Jacob, however, evolves quickly. He never harms a human or puts Bella in danger in spite of their tempestuous relationship.[71] Even though his wolf form emerges as a protective force against vampires, he establishes a working relationship with the Cullens.[72] He asserts himself as an Alpha leader to protect Bella and her child.[73] He and Edward reluctantly develop a relationship.[74] And after imprinting on Renesmee, Jacob shows a fiercely protective loyalty.[75] If his actions do not make clear his resolve to modify his behavior in ways that fit the circumstances, his words certainly do. When he finally understands that Bella will marry Edward, he reminds her of the story of King Solomon, the two women, and the baby in describing his willingness to walk away and not cause her any additional pain.[76] His ability to adapt to situations, to fight for who he loves, and to let go when he must all demonstrate how his exercising of his will defines who he is.

Perhaps of even greater import, Jacob attempts to push Bella into autonomy from Edward and into making her own choices. For example, when Jacob wants her to come to a bonfire party on the reservation, she tells him that she will ask, meaning she will ask Edward, not her father. Jacob's response highlights his discomfort with the control Edward exercises over her.[77] Like Edward, Jacob shows concern for Bella's safety, but he also wants her to think for herself and to choose with whom she spends time without having to sneak off,[78] run away,[79] or make elaborate arrangements.[80] He also challenges the absolute nature of her feelings for Edward and seeks to become a romantic option for her.[81] Part of his maturation includes making informed decisions about who he is, what he wants, and encouraging the same in others.

Similarly Edward, at least in some ways, is the ultimate case study in mastery of the physical body. As previously discussed, he controls his vampire hunger as a way to retain his ties to whatever humanity remains within him.[82] Consistently he chooses not to harm Bella, even when their first encounters threaten to overwhelm him. *Midnight Sun* reveals the extent of his pain when, at her scent, he plots the murder of a classroom filled with students to have her,[83] then contemplates her death along with an unfortunate office assistant,[84] and finally leaves home to avoid further temptation.[85] Moreover, the entire plot line of *New Moon* centers on his decision to leave Bella when he recognizes the constant danger his presence represents for her.[86]

Meyer goes to great lengths to present Edward as heroic and unselfish in his decision making with regard to Bella. He consistently attributes every action he takes as directly tied to a need to protect her, and his motivation becomes nothing less than his great love for her.[87] But at almost every turn, he seeks to define her options and to take away her ability to act for herself. For instance, she wants to become a vampire and for him to turn her; he demands a marriage she does not want as the price.[88] Her desire for sexual intimacy becomes his bargaining chip to get her to agree to this marital union instead of a sexual relationship being something he gives her willingly and without condition.[89] Perhaps most significantly, when she wants to keep her baby, she must turn to Rosalie to guarantee against Edward acting outside of her will and taking the baby without her permission.[90]

In this regard, a connection with Mormon teaching about Satan comes to the fore. Mormons teach that Satan becomes a problem precisely because he wants to remove free agency from humanity. The Book of Moses 4:1–4 states the issue clearly:

> 1 And I, the Lord God, spake unto Moses, saying: That Satan, whom thou hast commanded in the name of mine Only Begotten, is the same which was from the beginning, and he came before me, saying—Behold, here am I, send me, I will be thy son, and I will redeem all mankind, that one soul shall not be lost, and surely I will do it; wherefore give me thine honor.

> 2 But, behold, my Beloved Son, which was my Beloved and Chosen from the beginning, said unto me—Father, thy will be done, and the glory be thine forever.

> 3 Wherefore, because that Satan rebelled against me, and sought to destroy the agency of man, which I, the Lord God, had given him, and also, that I should give unto him mine own power; by the power of mine Only Begotten, I caused that he should be cast down;

> 4 And he became Satan, yea, even the devil, the father of all lies, to deceive and to blind men, and to lead them captive at his will, even as many as would not hearken unto my voice.

Satan's desire to save humankind comes at the price of removing a gift God gave to humanity: free choice. Compelling salvation, however, comes not out of concern for human souls and their fate, but rather to garner the glory due to God alone. Thus in one action, this story presents Satan as acting against what God designed and trying to earn praise through obligation as opposed to the kind of praise God desires: praise freely given.

Exercising one's freedom and independence to make choices functions to make a person more like God, according to LDS teaching. The capacity to weigh decisions and act on them should never seem routine as in following a checklist. Rather, each choice requires grappling with the consequences and understanding the potential outcomes. So for instance, when Edward tries to keep Bella from Jacob, she expresses his physically holding her back as an emotional barrier as well.[91] She needs to experience her love for Jacob and to comprehend how that love hurts him in order to grow up and see a world beyond Edward and to choose to be with Edward freely.[92]

Moreover, Mormons believe that to be hindered from making decisions for oneself equates to keeping a person away from developing his or her fullest potential. Again, Edward claims that he places priority on maintaining Bella's safety. But in doing so, he limits her possibilities. Thus, for example, with the family in danger, he cannot teach Bella, even though a new vampire, how to fight.[93] While her shield might prove beneficial to them all, it comes to Kate to push her to develop skills possibly of use against the Volturi.[94] Likewise, without her enlisting Rosalie to guard her, she would never have given birth to Renesmee. His desire to keep her safe actually squelches her ability to act for herself, her family, and her community. Until she breaks out on her own, she cannot live into her potential.

## Conclusions

Meyer's emphasis on choice in her books largely reflects Mormon teaching on moral agency, though other Christian traditions also hold up the importance of free will. Meyer contrasts the determinism common in teenaged perception and highlighted in all three lead characters' understanding of their worlds, with the more complex reality of understanding one's environment as responsive to the decisions one makes.

In this regard, Jacob actually emerges as an exemplar. Unlike Bella, who seems driven merely by her love for Edward into a series of actions that often do not regard the consequences for others, or Edward, who demonstrates great control of his self, but an inability to let Bella grow and change, Jacob matures from a young man caught up in the demands of his community to a man who can, and does, interact meaningfully with others. He reveals to Bella the complexity of the world she inhabits and pushes her to think beyond her wild abandon for Edward toward her responsibilities to her family, her friends, and to what it means to be a parent. He proves worthy again and again of overcoming what he thought of as destiny and forging a new way that both honors Bella and her child and respects others in his community and in once rival groups. Most significantly, he sees in Bella not someone fragile and in need of coddling, but someone strong and resourceful who must make her own way. In this sense, he stands out as a strong contrast to Edward, who never quite wants Bella that free.

## QUESTIONS TO CONSIDER

1. The relationship between Edward and Bella is supposed to serve as an exemple of the great love people can experience with a soul mate. To many readers, however, it functions as a love that removes possibilities from Bella: normal relationship with her family, more than one child, and her own human life. How do you assess their relationship? Is Edward a good and healthy choice for Bella or more of a dangerous addiction?

2. Mormon teaching holds that Satan seeks human salvation, but more for his own honor than for any concern for humanity itself. In reading Edward, do you see any parallels between the him and Satan? Although Edward professes to act solely out of concern for Bella, does he? Why or why not?

3. This chapter argues that of the three lead characters, Jacob demonstrates the most capacity for growth. Is he at an advantage by being the youngest of the three and the one undergoing the most transformations? Or is he favored because of a strong community that supports him in his changes?

# 5

# Renesmee

## Introduction

Renesmee, the unexpected and widely misunderstood daughter of a human Bella and a vampire Edward, makes her first appearance midway through *Breaking Dawn*—the fourth and final novel in the *Twilight* saga. To the vampire community, she appears an immortal child, turned when still young. Because of difficulties with the intersection of vampire powers and children's immaturity, the Volturi enforce a ban on the creation of such beings. In reality, a half-vampire, half-human hybrid, she possesses qualities of both parents and, in the narrative, arouses fierce protective instincts among the vampire, shape-shifter, and human groups she encounters.

Her unusual conception, remarkable gifts, and unique nature provide a strong basis for comparison to the stories relating the birth of Jesus in both the canonical and noncanonical gospels, as well as to teachings of the church on the dual nature of Christ. To label her a Christ figure overburdens an infant with too many expectations, given her mere weeks of life in the four-novel storyline. Nonetheless, even a cursory reading of her story demonstrates how Meyer plays on the story of Jesus to speak about Renesmee and her impact on the various beings around her. This chapter explores these connections, beginning with Renesmee's conception and Bella's pregnancy before turning to the threats against her young life. It then looks at her amazing precociousness and the relationship of such to her mixed nature.

## The Conception and Pregnancy

Early church documents do not place great emphasis on the issue of Jesus' conception or birth. Paul, for instance, the earliest and most prolific New Testament writer, never relays any stories of miraculous events, preferring to say merely that Christ was born of a woman (Gal. 4:4). This lack of reference to Christ's conception likely indicates that most first followers did not consider Christ's origins to be as significant as his death for the salvation of humanity. Nonetheless, the writers of the gospels of Matthew and Luke in the New Testament each include narratives about the conception and birth at the outset of their texts. Moreover, each struggles in its presentations with how to explain the life of a man both divine and human. The intermingling of these two distinctive types proved a kind of curiosity. How did it happen? What resulted? What signs of both parents can a person see in the child?

For these writers, if Jesus indeed came from God and existed as God's son in some sense other than via an adoption, then the question of Jesus' conception arises. To produce a child requires both sperm and egg and thus father and mother. Although both Matthew and Luke include a genealogical chart tracing descendants through the line of Joseph (Mt. 1:1–17; Lk. 3:23–38), each indicates that the child Mary carried actually belonged to the Holy Spirit (Mt. 1:18–21 and Lk. 1:30–35) and thus came somehow from God and not a human father. The "how" of the impregnation remains untold, and both accounts simply assume that God can make such an unusual birth happen regardless of the biological processes typically required.

By contrast, the story in *Breaking Dawn* focuses considerable attention on the details of Bella's conception, pregnancy, and delivery. The difference likely rests in that the resultant child, Renesmee, plays a significant role in the story as a threat to Bella's life. Further, her impact on how the narrative unfolds occurs while she remains an infant, as opposed to her developing into a more noteworthy adult character. Most significantly, the question of her nature directly affects how the story progresses.

*Breaking Dawn* characterizes Bella's conception of a child as a complete surprise to all of the parties involved. When Bella and Edward go on their honeymoon, no one anticipates the need for birth control in that no stories of humans surviving such an intimate encounter with a vampire exist. Additionally, the possibility of a resultant pregnancy never came to mind since vampires do not reproduce.[1] This cross-species impregnation requires the ability of Bella's human body to change in order to support a pregnancy. By contrast, no one knew male vampires possessed viable, if somewhat altered, sperm, as the frozen-in-time bodies of female vampires could not develop in such a way as to give birth. Thus, shortly after the consummation of the marriage Bella begins to experience unusual hunger,[2] physical exhaustion, strange dreams,[3] and revulsion toward some food.[4] After performing calculations with regard to her menstrual cycle, she reaches the logical conclusion.[5]

Meyer chooses to emphasize the uniqueness of the child in terms of the strangeness of Bella's experience, beginning with what occurs in her body. The point of conception and the onset of symptoms come in much too rapid a succession.[6] Bella notes, for instance, an almost immediate change in the contour of her abdomen—something far more typical of a third or fourth month in a typical human pregnancy—and she feels the baby moving in that same short time frame.[7] The fetus also presents an ongoing threat to her life. Requiring different nutritional resources than Bella can provide,[8] she must drink blood to assuage the baby's hunger.[9] Further, the fetus's strength breaks Bella's bones.[10] And the few stories the Cullens can discover about such births describe the children as eating their way out of their mothers, killing them in the process.[11] Indeed, the bodily struggle Bella endures makes her appear on the way to a quick death to all who see her.[12]

By contrast, the gospels say little about Mary's pregnancy, and thus readers assume it to be normal. Other signs, however, point out the unusual nature of the child. Each text, for instance, opens by making reference to some atypical and dramatic births in order to emphasize something out of the ordinary in Jesus' beginnings. In Luke the story of Elizabeth, Mary's cousin, comes first and relates how a seemingly barren older woman (Lk. 1:7) enjoys the opportunity to have a child and demonstrate the blessing of God to a community that saw her as disgraced (Lk. 1:25). Matthew opens with a genealogy that includes four women—Tamar, Rahab, Ruth, and Bathsheba (Mt. 1:1–7). A woman who posed as a prostitute to get pregnant by her father-in-law, a prostitute, a foreigner, and an adulteress seem unlikely candidates for inclusion in the line of the savior, but each demonstrates how remarkable figures often emerge from unusual circumstances.

Although the gospel stories around Mary's conception differ in many respects from Bella's tale, the narratives converge in some unanticipated ways. According to the gospel of Luke, Mary receives a visitation from the angel Gabriel announcing her selection to give birth to the son of God, even though she remained virginal (Lk. 1:26–35). As with Bella, Mary does not understand the "how" of the process, given that nothing in her experience or in the typical experience of humans prepared her for such a moment. Moreover, the gospel of Matthew portrays Joseph, Mary's betrothed husband, as reacting to Mary's pregnancy by wanting to divorce quickly and quietly to avoid scandal (Mt. 1:18–20). His reaction as a man reflects something similar to Edward's response in terms of wanting to take an immediate step to rectify what he defines as a problem.[13] Further, back in Luke, Mary chooses to bond with her cousin Elizabeth, also pregnant, to receive encouragement (Lk. 1:39–44). Similarly, Bella seeks out female support in Rosalie, Edward's "sister," because in Rosalie's fierce desire for a child she could not carry, Bella knew she would defend her from Edward and his desire to terminate the pregnancy.[14] This natural alliance of women seems a world away from the men, especially Edward and Jacob, who cannot fathom what they see as Bella's "extreme" connection to this child.[15]

In the end, both the gospels and *Breaking Dawn* want to point to the special qualities of these half-human, half-other children by focusing on the experience of their mothers. Even though they go about it quite distinctly, the point remains that their unique natures defy normal circumstances with regard to even the fundamentals of the birth process. Both Jesus and Renesmee, in this context, challenge what one expects from the moment of their conceptions forward, as one might anticipate with children of such rare pedigrees. Further, their stories outline the impact on parents who come into the situation unaware and even unprepared to understand what exactly having such an exceptional child entails. This feature makes their stories work for readers who know something of what it means to bring a child into a family but also struggle to realize the full impact on their lives of having such an infant.

## Gathering Threats

Following the birth of Jesus, the gospel of Matthew relates almost immediate peril to the child in the form of Herod the Great. In this story, Herod becomes fearful when he hears about the birth of the true King of the Jews[16] (Mt. 2:2). To assure himself that no rival exists, he orders the slaughter of all male children under the age of two (Mt. 2:16–18). This accounting of events finds no basis in any historical record.[17] Rather, it fits with the writer of Matthew's idea of Jesus in the mold of Moses. Moses, of course, faced a similar threat from the unnamed Pharaoh in the book of Exodus (Ex. 1:22). But the story told in Matthew does reflect the paranoid nature of Herod known to scholars of the period.[18] Likewise, in Meyer's book, Renesmee stands immediately in danger from the Volturi after her birth. This ruling group forbade the turning of children into vampires because they could not develop a maturity appropriate for control over their impulses to kill. Throughout the course of history, the frequent rampages of such vampire children caused disruption in the human community and brought unwelcome attention to vampires.[19] As a result, any vampire who produced such "offspring," and perhaps even those vampires with knowledge of one or association with its creator, was executed.[20]

When the vampire Irina sees Renesmee from a distance and assumes her to be an immortal child, she reports this violation to the Volturi, who plan to come after the Cullens.[21] As in the biblical story of Herod the Great, the consequences for the child (and in this case the family) prove dire. The biblical story recounts that Herod unilaterally issues his decree. So also the Volturi come to Forks to remove the problem and any associated threat to the vampire community.[22] No opportunity exists to plead for the lives of the children killed in the gospel of Matthew, and no chance for trial or even negotiation is offered by the Volturi. Moreover, unlike Joseph and Mary, who flee to Egypt for refuge (Mt. 2:13–14), Edward and Bella cannot run to a safe haven.[23] Thus the Cullens prepare for a confrontation with the Volturi by calling in witnesses to attempt to sway the rulers away from a death sentence.[24]

## An Amazing Child

The story of the young Renesmee also bears some resemblance to two narratives in Luke. According to this gospel, shortly after the birth of Jesus, his parents take the child to Jerusalem for presentation in the temple (Lk. 2:22–24). A second story recounts his coming to the temple as a young boy of twelve (Lk. 2:41–49). On both occasions, Jesus proves amazing to persons associated with this important site. Simeon, a devout man, sees in the infant Jesus the Messiah (Lk. 2:25–35), as does the prophet Anna (Lk. 2:36–38). Both see in him salvation for humanity (2:29–32 and 2:38). Similarly, the young man Jesus sits with the teachers and stuns them with his insights (Lk. 2:46–47). In like fashion, Meyer presents Renesmee as provoking an intense reaction among all she encounters. Her ability to show people images of what she knows mesmerizes almost every being she touches.[25]

Such stories, even in their brevity, demonstrate how the special child's contact with others reveals his or her's importance. The gospels look beyond Joseph and Mary, who set paradigms for the appropriate reaction to such a turn of events. For instance, Elizabeth experiences a leaping feeling from her child *in utero* when Mary comes to visit (Lk. 1:41). Wise men appear offering homage to this new king based on their observation of the heavens and a new star (Mt. 2:2). Shepherds travel to the birth site following the direction of angels (Lk. 2:8–18). And as noted, temple personnel understand the import of both the infant and the young man in their environs.

Renesmee similarly gathers a disparate community to her for support and defense. Like the reaction of John the Baptist as a fetus to the child Mary carries, so Jacob responds with a powerful and inexplicable attachment to a pregnant Bella.[26] While he initially attributes it to his ongoing love for her,[27] he imprints on the newborn Renesmee and thus eventually understands that his draw to the infant began even before her birth.[28] The wolf shape-shifters, once determined to destroy the fetus as a perceived threat,[29] support Jacob and rise up on her behalf in the face of the Volturi.[30] Even other vampires, generally not committed to assisting others of their kind, stand ready to protect her once they witness her remarkable nature.[31] Her allure also extends to the human community. Charlie, Bella's father, may not fully understand the circumstances of her life, but he nonetheless finds himself immediately enthralled.[32]

In both the gospels and *Breaking Dawn*, family focus rests on the arrival and subsequent safety of the child. While those persons closest naturally observe the uniqueness of what happens before them, characters with a different, less direct perspective on the events unfolding demonstrate the power of its draw too. Not every baby is greeted with a coterie of wise men or shepherds as in the gospels. Not every child draws attention in the temple of wise and respected adults. These encounters remind Jesus' parents of the import of their child. In *Breaking Dawn*, the baby's importance also involves others' actions to shape reaction to her. Through the eyes of the gathered witnesses, Renesmee emerges as someone different, special, and utterly out of the ordinary.[33] Moreover, because potential enemies encounter her as a child, something far less threatening unfolds. How much harm, after all, could one so young inflict?

## The Infancy Gospel of Thomas

Among the surviving noncanonical literature, the second-century document known as *The Infancy Gospel of Thomas* stands out for its unique take on the life of Christ. It focuses on stories about Jesus as a child and attempts to depict the events of his life between his birth and his public ministry. Of even greater interest, it explores what it might mean if a child possessed the abilities of a deity and the self-knowledge of one's self as such. This pursuit makes it more like Meyer's presentation of Renesmee in *Breaking Dawn*. Both examine, in their own ways, how the extraordinariness of a previously unknown type of human gets expressed in the guise of a young child.

In *The Infancy Gospel of Thomas*, Jesus does not win any behavioral awards. For instance, when the son of a scholar named Annas drains a pool of water he collected or when a young boy accidentally bumps into him, Jesus curses them both and they die (3:2–3; 4:1–2). After the parents of the second victim complain, and Joseph, Jesus' father, speaks to him, Jesus strikes his accusers blind (5:2). Nor does Jesus accept the rebuke of Joseph. The words recorded sound much like the angry exclamations of any bratty child: "Don't you know that I don't really belong to you? Don't make me upset"(5:6). But Jesus also manages to perform some remarkable feats. He raises a child from the dead (albeit to defend himself, 9:4–5).[34] Work he undertakes in the fields produce a remarkable yield (12:1–4), and he assists his father in the carpentry shop, including stretching the wood to make it even (12:1–4). He also amazes many teachers (see chapters 6, 7, 14, 19), although he puts at least one in his place (chapter 15).

All of these stories demonstrate that as with most children, ability does not necessarily coincide with maturity. Even as the son of God, Jesus is presented here as precocious, and still too young to understand how to react appropriately in particular circumstances. Bursts of temper and self-centeredness simply underscore what parents already know about raising a child. Similarly, a powerful Renesmee must receive instruction to not always act on instinct. For instance, when she meets her human grandfather Charlie for the first time, she must be told to keep her gifts (and her bite!) to herself.[35] No matter how remarkable her powers, she cannot understand without explanation the complexity of her life and familial circumstances. Additionally, she demonstrates the selfishness of a young child with regard to Jake. From her perspective, he belongs to her alone, and she wants to keep him around for her purposes much like a child refuses to share a toy.[36] Whatever "imprinting" might entail, she only can process it at her young age, and that means simply knowing "Jake=Mine."

Again, as with the birth accounts, these stories attempt to place all of the attendant powers of such special children in typical behavioral patterns. Such treatment stresses the humanity of the character for the reader. If one could not understand how Mary and Joseph raised the son of God in their home (or how Bella and Edward coped with a half-human, half-vampire child), the likeness to any childrearing conundrums makes it easier to grasp. Therein rests the power of the narratives. The extraordinary remains, but it comes in a guise any parent could process readily.

### The Question of Nature

Naturally the theologians of the early church also thought far more rigorously and systematically about the dual nature of Christ than some of the biblical writers. Most famously, the issue arose in a controversy called Arianism in the early fourth century. Just as the Roman emperors turned to Christianity as a faith, the issue of how Jesus related to God set off a firestorm. Different schools of thought on this question threatened to split the church right down the middle. After a brief exploration of the details of this crisis, a comparison to how the church understood the nature of Jesus and how Meyer portrays Renesmee's nature will follow.

A bishop in the Egyptian city of Alexandria, Arius sought to understand the origins of Jesus. In his study of scripture, Arius concluded that prior to his incarnation as a human, Jesus existed as a divine being. However, Arius also believed that God created the Son and thus, at some point, God existed, but the Christ did not. Contemporary Trinitarian Christians likely never considered the issue. But given that the biblical material itself does not define the relationship between God, the Christ, and the Holy Spirit, this question proved of some import to those church leaders struggling to understand the nature of God and the connections between God, Jesus, and the Holy Spirit. The teachings of Arius in particular set in motion a drive for some consensus among early Christians about this issue.

Arius's teachings proved controversial. After objections from some local opponents in and around Alexandria, the bishop of the region, Alexander, attempted to get Arius and some of his followers to sign a Confession on Orthodoxy. They refused, and the church excommunicated them. But the controversy did not die down, and thus the emperor Constantine supported the first ecumenical council at Nicea in 325 C.E., where officials representing various Christian communities gathered for discussion of such topics. At that meeting the delegates forming a majority defined God and Christ as "homoousious," or of the same substance, and produced the Nicene Creed, which declares the same. The opening lines read: "We believe in one God, the Father Almighty, Maker of all things visible and invisible. And in one Lord Jesus Christ, the Son of God, begotten of the Father [the only-begotten; that is, of the essence of the Father, God of God], Light of Light, very God of very God, begotten, not made, being of one substance with the Father." The controversy, however, continued even after the death of Arius, and another council at Constantinople (381) continued the discussion, refined the creed, and added the complicated question of the Holy Spirit to the mix. In the end, however, the Trinitarians carried the day and the history of the church.

Any life as unusual as the one that Christians claim for Christ evokes questions. Meyer plays on that theme with the nature of Renesmee, a child of some mystery to her family and the larger communities with which she interacts. As half-human and half-vampire, Renesmee provokes questions about her identity, which concern both her family and others. For instance, as mentioned previously, the Cullens must act quickly to understand her condition, given that her rapid development and nutritional needs *in utero,* and the method of her delivery, all threaten her mother's life. The accelerated physical growth continues following her birth, and the family starts a program of regular measurement to assess it.[37] Renesmee also demonstrates mental acuity, as she speaks in perfect and complete sentences.[38] Only when they discover a similar child in South America, Nahuel, does it become clear that Renesmee's physical maturation will slow. Further, Nahuel teaches them that she will continue to live more like a vampire with regard to immortality, although her gender likely renders her unable to turn a human into a vampire.[39]

As with the controversy over Jesus, questions about Renesmee threaten to cause some disruptions in a number of quarters. The wolf shape-shifters, for example, fear her before her birth and want to eliminate her by killing Bella. As a group, they exist in order to protect humans from vampires, and she represents a potential breach in the safety of the area over which they maintain responsibility.[40] This decision for action against her leads Jacob and his followers, Seth and Leah, to break from the pack in a kind of excommunication in order to protect a pregnant Bella.[41]

The Volturi also arrive on the scene after hearing of the presence of an immortal child. As with other vampires the Cullens gathered as witnesses, all must be taught to recognize her mixed nature by observing things like her heartbeat,[42] the blood in her cheeks,[43] and her remarkable growth.[44] Even then, however, the issue of her development remains unresolved, and Aro proposes a future council to assess how this blending of human and vampire progresses.[45] As with the early Christian community, trying to define something previously unknown challenges all previous norms and arouses controversy. A gathering of officials serves to construct an orthodoxy that, in the case of Nicea and Constantinople, regularizes definitions of the relationship of the Father, Son, and Spirit while also supporting the growth of a unified church under the auspices of Rome. In the case of *Breaking Dawn*, the Cullens and the Volturi both strive to control the definitions put on Renesmee and thus determine her fate, that of her family, and of the future of the vampire community. In this case, the witness of another hybrid child, Nahuel, offers the necessary standard and earns the Cullen's safety.[46]

## Conclusions

In spite of the cultural celebrations of Christmas as a holiday filled with joy, "the Gospel birth narratives are far from feel-good stories. They tell of a family outcast and exiled, hunted and rejected. They tell of children killed, of a sword pierced to a mother's heart, of a judgment on the nations."[47] While they attempt to puzzle out the conundrum of a hybrid child—half human and half divine—they leave significant gaps in understanding the nature of such a child or what it meant in terms of his power. Other documents, like *The Infancy Gospel of Thomas*, attempt to fill in holes in the childhood experience of such a creature, while The Nicene Creed works to spell out with some precision the implications of the nature of this new being.

Meyer covers much of the same territory in her final book with Renesmee. She explores the horrifying impact of a difficult pregnancy and birth on a family, of the opposition to such a child from varied communities, and of the struggle to understand the dual nature of the infant. But, as in the birth stories of Jesus, what exactly results from this unusual combination remains largely unknown. Even the appearance of another such child cannot account for what Renesmee might become or what impact she might wield inside a family that lives differently from most of their kind. Moreover, the unique gifts she possesses have only begun to show their power at such an early life stage. Where her story might go and what she might accomplish remain just as much a mystery as her miraculous origin.

## QUESTIONS TO CONSIDER

1. What do you see in the birth stories of Jesus and Renesmee that explains how two different natures coincide in one form? Are birth stories a helpful venue for addressing such concerns? Why or why not?

2. The Volturi use Renesmee as a pretext for a confrontation with the Cullens. Even in the face of evidence that she is not a violation of their laws, they persist in trying to define her in such a way as to neutralize the impact of this family on the vampire world. Do you see any similarities in the attempts of ecumenical councils to control the definition of the relationship between God and Christ? What is at stake in the outcome of such a process?

3. What does it mean to be a hybrid or a cross between two disparate types of being? How can the joining of two forms in one body serve as an example of the possibilities of what can happen in communities struggling with how to mediate differences?

# 6

# Revelation, the Final Apocalypse, and the Coming of the Kingdom

## Introduction

The final book of the New Testament canon—the book of Revelation—envisions human history coming to a decisive and violent end as the kingdom of God arrives in all of its fullness. In its portrayal of the dramatic confrontation between the forces of good and the powers of evil, it introduces language such as "apocalypse" and "Armageddon" that continues to resonate in the modern cultural imagination. But the book also maintains a reputation for confounding many of its readers with its strange imagery, its symbolic names, numbers, and colors, and its memorable cast of characters. Even many Christians fail to understand this unique piece of literature within their scriptural tradition precisely because the text's bizarre nature resulted in an interpretive tradition often as mystifying as the book itself.

No final conclusion to a historical epoch comes in the *Twilight* saga. Nor does Meyer make use of bizarre and often mystifying imagery to relate her ending. Nonetheless, she does borrow some thematic characteristics of John's Revelation to bring her story to a close. This chapter uses the book of Revelation as a touchstone to talk about how Meyer presents the Volturi in *New*

*Moon, Eclipse,* and *Breaking Dawn* and how their conflict with the Cullen family mimics many of the qualities of the Christian biblical text's ultimate conclusion. Beginning with an examination of the kind of menace the Volturi represent and how they exercise their control, this chapter accounts for similarities between the Volturi and John's presentation of Satan, Rome, and Rome's leadership in Revelation. It then proceeds to a reading of the final conflict and the anticipated results. Comparison to the preparation for the last battle over Jerusalem will emerge here. A consideration of how the showdown with the Volturi fizzles will also stand against the lack of the expected bloodbath in the biblical texts. Finally, the chapter will detail how the Cullens embody something similar to John's presentation of the Christian community and, as such, become ultimate victors through their use of nonviolent resistance.

### The Volturi

Readers first meet the Volturi in Meyer's books as friends of Carlisle during his early years as a vampire.[1] When first mentioned in *Twilight,* Bella observes a painting of them as almost godlike in appearance, and Edward notes their patronage of the arts and their almost aristocratic bearing. They even receive praise as the cornerstone of a system of justice that produces a kind of lawful peace in the vampire community.[2] Over the course of the books, however, hints about a more troubling nature arise. Edward, for instance, in *New Moon* describes the likelihood of his killing himself if Bella dies and sees raising the ire of the Volturi as a sure way to end his existence.[3] Alice affirms such a fear when he later attempts to actualize his own demise and she explains how they function as a much-revered ruling family who enforce a code of conduct on the larger community.[4] Their abilities as enforcers take on more frightening dimensions as their guard appears. Jane, for example, wields the power of pain;[5] Alec removes all physical sensation;[6] and Chelsea either strengthens or breaks the ties between vampires.[7]

At first glance, these vampires appear quite different from Satan and his servants in the book of Revelation. The dragon (or Satan) comes to earth after losing a heavenly conflict (Rev. 12:7–9). Angry and still wanting to act against the deity, it attempts to destroy Christians (Rev. 17:13–17). Two beasts assist in the effort. One, Rome and its emperors, appears with ten horns and seven heads (Rev. 13:1). A second, likely associated with the imperial cult (Rev. 13:11), serves at the will of the first and sometimes gets called the false prophet (Rev. 16:13; 19:20; and 20:10). Finally, the whore of Babylon—or city of Rome—appears as a wildly attired woman drinking the blood of saints for her amusement (Rev. 17:1–6). Designed to convey the real threats to some Christians in the Roman Empire, these remarkable figures function to conjure horror and fear.

While Meyer's work lacks the strange symbolism of Revelation, some commonalities nonetheless come across thematically. For instance, just as Aro, Marcus and Caius—the three main brothers of the family—possess a kind of beauty and elegance, so also does Satan enjoy a rather illustrious beginning that points to a striking nature. Revelation 12:9 indicates Satan existed in the divine realm and lured to his service a coterie of angels. The wording of the passage juxtaposes Michael, an archangel, and his angels with Satan and his, suggesting that Satan himself was an angel (Rev. 12:7–9).[8] In fact, "the legend of the rebellion and expulsion of Lucifer, as formulated by Jewish and Christian writers, describes Lucifer as the chief in the hierarchy of heaven, and preeminent among all created beings in beauty, power, and wisdom."[9] But just as Bella cannot determine if the appearance of the brothers qualifies as beautiful,[10] so also does Satan begin to take on a more ominous and less pleasing guise as the embodiment of evil.[11] The attractiveness becomes tarnished by the actions of Satan; fear of the Volturi make them simultaneously fascinating and repulsive.

Bella, the narrator and thus primary source of information in these novels, only knows that the Volturi harmed Edward,[12] threatened her life,[13] and stand ready to destroy her family.[14] Thus, whatever positive they might possibly embody fades in comparison to their ability to cause injury or death. In this manner, they resemble John's idea of Rome as the locus of evil in the book of Revelation. For the most part, the Roman Empire generated positive results for those areas that fell under its rule. The protection extended by the army, the construction of roads and the resultant extension of commerce, and the freedom to practice one's own religion stand out as benefits of life under Rome's control.[15] But for the community John addresses, the excesses of Nero (and then, later, the practices of Domitian) and the localized persecution of Christians in the city itself made life tenuous at best as Roman rule became oppressive and deadly.[16]

In this manner, Rome demonstrates the kind of power that Satan and his servants hold over humanity. Appearing larger than life to the people under its rule, the beast enters this drama by rising from the sea (Rev. 13:1). In apocalyptic literature, the sea stands for the uncontrollable, the abyss that requires a divine hand to tame. In discussing the created order, Jon Levenson notes how the biblical text reflects ancient Mesopotamian creation as combat myths where God must defeat the forces of chaos embodied in the sea, such as the great sea monster Leviathan.[17] The emergence of this beast in Revelation goes back to that time and raises alarm among its readers that a primordial revolution against the divine power threatens them. This beast, however, evokes more than the distant beginnings of all things, it also plays on more recent history. One of the heads of the beast, for example, "seemed to have received a death-blow, but its mortal wound had been healed" (Rev. 13:3). This symbol represents Nero, the Roman emperor who committed suicide in 68 C.E. Rumors persisted throughout the region during the time of this text's composition that he had returned from the dead. If, indeed, the beast held even the power of life and death, the community facing it stood no chance. In Revelation, humans thus worship the beast because of its great power; "Who is like the beast, and who can fight against it?" (Rev. 13:4).

Similarly, when the Volturi arrive in all of their majesty at the end of *Breaking Dawn*, they come in an unbroken black line emerging almost magically from the trees with feet never seeming to touch the snowy ground.[18] As with the beast's entrance, their appearance suggests something undefeatable to Bella, who sees no hope for the Cullens and their allies in this confrontation.[19] The Volturi possess too many advantages. First, vampires already fear them. Alice tells Bella that no one challenges them because the Volturi always come out on top.[20] When they threaten the Cullens, none of them (or their vampire friends) believe they can fight and win.[21] Second, their numbers alone secure their position.[22] Finally, they present a formidable array of both offensive and defensive skills from Aro's ability to read thoughts, Jane's mental burning, Alec's sensory deprivation, Demetri's tracking, and Renata's shield. Bella notes, for example, how once Aro touches Edward, he accesses every strategy the group planned.[23]

In Revelation, the power of life and death rests with Satan and the beast, as well as with the whore of Babylon. The beast, for instance, receives power over the Christian community to conquer (Rev. 13:7) and even to kill (Rev. 13:10) them. The second beast, or the false prophet, compels people to bow down to the beast under the threat of death (Rev. 13:15). Perhaps most memorably, the whore sits on the mighty waters drunk on the blood of Christians (Rev. 17:6). Likewise, Meyer gives the Volturi the power of life and death. In *New Moon*, for example, as Bella, Edward, and Alice leave their audience with Aro and his brothers, a group of tourists arrives, unaware that they will soon serve as food for the family and their guard.[24] Similarly, in *Eclipse,* Jane, Felix and a small contingent of Volturi arrive to deal with the issue of the newborn vampires, but come after the completion of the battle. The Cullens capture Bree, and Carlisle wants to teach rather than to kill her. But Jane shows no mercy as a sign of their power.[25] Likewise, Irina dies quickly in *Breaking Dawn* for passing on misinformation to the family and then for showing defiance.[26]

The Christian audience of Revelation and the reading audience of the *Twilight* saga naturally root for the underdogs, given the presentation of the ruling power as an enemy that threatens the existence of each text's heroes. Any positive aspects of Roman rule or of Volturi control are lost in the confrontation between a beleaguered Christian community and Rome's powerful emperors or the Cullens against the vampire elite. But both also show notable vulnerabilities. In the biblical text, Rome needs the resources of its subjects to survive and their loyalty to maintain its dominance and does what is necessary to acquire both. Likewise, the Volturi keep their position by consistently annihilating or annexing any threats and thus generating fear in those vampires over whom they hold sway.

### Acquisition

In Revelation, Rome controls the world John describes and his audience understands that living in the Roman Empire meant acceding to the demands of imperial rule. As the text says of the beast, "it was given authority over every tribe and people and language and nation, and all of the inhabitants of the earth will worship it, everyone whose name has not been written from the foundation of the world in the book of life of the Lamb that was slaughtered" (Rev. 13:7b–8). While Revelation continues to talk about the beast marking people with its number in order to assure that it controls all of their commerce (Rev. 13:16–17), other requirements included paying taxes, supplying crops, service in varied forms of labor, and participation in rituals related to the state/cult.[27] Further, to consolidate its hold over a region, Rome often co-opted local elites into service. For example, in Jerusalem, the temple functioned as the locus for imperial domination, as it had during the occupation of the Persians and the Greeks in centuries previous.[28] By enlisting the aid of and controlling the priestly aristocracy, the Romans assure that key leadership in a region remains loyal to them and thus squelch the best equipped for any real opposition.

The way Meyer depicts the Volturi corresponds to this idea of the Roman Empire. Eleazar, a vampire friend of the Cullens, once belonged to this elite group. He explains what he perceives to motivate their attack against this family as typical of their actions in the past. They act to acquire talent.[29] Alice's ability to see the future, Edward's gift for reading minds, and Bella's shielding of all outside influences intrigue Aro. But they also, if used against him, could potentially threaten the Volturi's position in the vampire world. If, however, the Volture spare the Cullens and others, such as Benjamin with his ability to manipulate natural elements, or Kate who can issue an electrical shock to attackers, they neutralize any opposition while gaining valuable resources in their own guard.[30]

## GIFTS AND TALENTS

According to Mormon teaching, persons moving from their pre-mortal existence to the human realm bring with them gifts and talents. "In mortality every person is endowed with spiritual gifts and talents that are part of their divine nature that can be refined, developed, and enlarged as a result of their earthly experiences" (Craig H. Hart, "Speeches: Our Divine Nature and Life Decisions," www.byub.org/talks/Download.aspx?id=59&md=pdf, 4). Such gifts assist humans in negotiating the challenges of an earthly life successfully. Likewise, Carlisle believes that the unique talents each vampire possesses come directly from tendencies already manifest in their human lives—only in the vampire manifestation, they become stronger (Meyer, *Twilight*, 307). Aro seems to share this view (Meyer, *Breaking Dawn*, 605). In her presentation of such gifts, Meyer follows the Mormon teaching that certain traits and talents are intrinsic to an individual and can be used for good purposes when applied well.

The acquisitive strategy generally comes into play at criminal trials where the Volturi appear to preserve order. As they execute a sentence, they perceive repentance among some and "kindly" offer amnesty (life) to the vampire or vampires with the skill they seek. Thus, they seem magnanimous in their justice. The vampire then joins the guard and enjoys a prestigious position with this leading group.[31] Their actions spark a loyalty to the family, ensured by the gifts of Chelsea to make one feel bonded.[32] Although Revelation lacks images for such a process of acquisition, it does encourage resistance to collaboration. Receiving the mark and worshiping the beast are equated with defiance of God (Rev. 13:6–8). Thus, persons conducting commerce with Rome or refusing to participate in the required public signs of allegiance risked their own lives, and Revelation calls on them to endure (Rev. 13:9–10) even if their own death results. Likewise, the Cullens understand that their only hope for survival comes in standing up against the Volturi, although it likely will lead to their destruction.[33]

### The Great Battle

The term *Armageddon* produces visions of a violent and decisive end to history when spoken in political and popular culture. Ronald Reagan, for example, wrote in his journal every day during his presidency and worried about various Middle Eastern crises. On May 15, 1981, he penned: "I wonder if we are destined to witness Armageddon."[34] The *Left Behind* series of sixteen novels retells the events of the book of Revelation, including Armageddon, in fictional form and presents it as a battle of the world's armies united against Israel. After the attacks on the United States on September 11, 2001, an "Armageddon" plan designed to make certain the government functioned during a nuclear attack went active.[35] Moreover, numerous movies, video games, music, and books carry this title or talk about Armageddon,[36] Y2K touched off fears of such an end, and even World Wrestling Entertainment produced a pay-per-view special in December 2008 with this name to denote a final showdown.

The term itself comes from Revelation 16:16, where the writer John describes the assembly of armies to fight against God in the last, epic battle. The name appears to combine the Hebrew word for hill (har) with the city of Megiddo, a great crossroads in Israel where many armies engaged over the centuries of its history. But the conflict that ensues proves short-lived at best. Revelation 19:11–21 speaks of the armies of heaven capturing the beast and the false prophet and defeating the kings of the earth. After a thousand-year prison sentence, Satan emerges and surrounds Jerusalem with an army (Rev. 20:7–9a). No battle ensues. Rather God simply destroys enemies by fire (Rev. 20:7b) and Satan gets thrown into the lake of fire and sulfur for eternity (Rev. 20:10). What appeared so enormous a threat to the community actually proved in the end not much of a challenge to God, who wins the contest easily. Moreover, the ultimate enemy of God, the last defeated, proves not to be the beast or even Satan. The most powerful opposition comes from Death and Hades. But after they release those persons whom they hold in bondage for judgment, they too are thrown into the lake of fire (Rev. 20:13–15) without much of a contest.

On the surface, the final "battle" between the Cullens and the Volturi may seem to lack the drama of the story in Revelation. However, several striking similarities emerge. For example, Satan and the beast produce demonic emissaries to gather the kings of the earth to wage war (Rev. 16:13–14). No word appears about the preparatory efforts of the divine forces, but the armies of heaven come out primed for battle (Rev. 19:14). Likewise, in *Breaking Dawn,* when Alice gets her vision of the Volturi coming to destroy the Cullens, they immediately begin to strategize and send out messengers to bring in their friends and potential allies to serve as witnesses, not combatants.[37] They also engage in basic training in order to counter possible challenges and to fight, if required.[38] Once the Volturi arrive, it becomes apparent they have mustered their own group of observers to attest to the justice of their actions.[39] But as Edward subsequently indicates, they typically did not expect to meet any force equal to their own[40] and thus likely did not engage in any special preparations for a fight.

The anticipated battle also becomes a non-event in Meyer's story. The Volturi arrive prepared to kill,[41] but leave defeated.[42] Only Irina loses her life for her witness against them. Given that they do not end up eternally in a lake of fire, completely destroyed, the comparison to Revelation might seem lost, but consider how the Cullens achieve their victory.

The armies of heaven in the book of Revelation fight behind a presence described both as a slain Lamb (see, for instance Rev. 5:6 and 17:14) and a rider called Faithful and True on a white horse garbed only in a robe dripping blood (Rev. 19:11–13). Clearly the figure of Christ, he also is described as white-haired with fiery eyes with a sharp sword for a tongue (Rev. 1:11–16). Although possessing the power of God, this Son reminds readers of Jesus executed by the Romans on a cross. The Christian community, of course, holds that he overcame death. But the power of his action comes not in a triumphant resurrection, but in what looked like defeat hanging dead on a cross. Moreover, this figure conquers not by the sword, but by the Word. For a community facing annihilation, then, the witness of its leader comes in accepting death fully confident that it does not represent a definitive end, and in speech as opposed to physical force. In other words, they cannot defeat the Romans in a battle and thus must use other weapons. Warren Carter points out that Christianity in its early years presented a not so obvious challenge to Rome. He writes:

> Parts of the early Christian movement (and texts) did challenge the empire and expose its vulnerability, but not by using military force, economic tactics such as withholding taxes and tribute, or political maneuvers such as assassination and intra-aristocratic conflict. Rather, the Christians presented an alternative social organization and a persuasive theological worldview...Using opportunities featured by the empire itself (education, literacy, travel, trade networks), some early Christians created an alternative, inclusive, and egalitarian social organization and meaning system that redefined the relationship of ruler to ruled.[43]

The Cullens perform similar maneuvers on the Volturi to achieve their success. Instead of plotting a fight they know they cannot win, they hope merely to cause the Volturi to pause and thus to gain an opportunity to present their case.[44] When their strategy works, they take the chance to demonstrate that Renesmee was born half-human and half-vampire rather than created an immortal child.[45] Although the Volturi still subtly attempt an attack, Bella's shield defends against them. Still, the Cullens do not go on the offense.[46] In other words, they embody passive resistance even though prepared to fight to their own death. Their strength comes from the integrity of their actions not simply in this situation, but in their way of life. Therein the real challenge to the Volturi appears. As Garrett sums up in his defense of the Cullens, their choice to live on animal blood, what he calls "the peaceful character of this life of sacrifice"[47] allows them to bond as a family, not only with other vampires but also with the humans and shape-shifters. By presenting an alternative social order, they embody the possibilities of living not as isolated predators always seeking advantage to meet their own needs, but as full members of a community characterized by love of one another. Their vampire witnesses see and know them over the course of their time together and learn to respect what they achieve, including their relationships with the Quileute and other humans. This new model of existence, then, plants the seeds that truly could undermine the hold of the Volturi on the vampire world.

### The Peaceable Kingdom

The book of Revelation concludes with the arrival of a new heaven and a new earth where God will dwell with those persons judged worthy for all eternity (Rev. 21:1–4). After enduring such an incredible trial, the image of a perfect home where God takes care of every need and no harm can come to the faithful, proved an incredible image of hope for persecuted Christians. A great and final reckoning by God determined an individual's qualifications for inclusion in this community, and the text sets up the criteria for acceptance as one's works (Rev. 20:12).

Meyer does not usher in a new or even a renewed Forks at the conclusion of *Breaking Dawn*. Indeed, for her, the Volturi depart cowed, but not defeated. The Cullens anticipate another confrontation will happen eventually.[48] No deity comes to live with them. No place of absolute perfection, free from pain or sorrow, emerges. But something important does happen. The bonds that the Cullens forged, among themselves and with other vampires, with the Quileute, and with other humans such as Charlie, do not disappear with the absence of a threat. Rather, the Cullens now stand ready to enjoy life in a community unlike any ever known.

In describing what cultural critics label the peaceable kingdom, the writer of Isaiah 11:6–9 says:

> The wolf shall live with the lamb,
> the leopard shall lie down with the kid,
> the calf and the lion and the fatling together,
> and a little child shall lead them.
> The cow and the bear shall graze,
> their young shall lie down together;
> and the lion shall eat straw like the ox.

The nursing child shall play over the hole of the asp,
   and the weaned child shall put his hand over the adder's
   den.
They will not hurt or destroy
   on all my holy mountain;
for the earth will be full of the knowledge of the Lord
   as the waters cover the sea.

This text imagines a place where natural enemies coexist without stress or strain, and where the things of God prevail over natural instincts to war. Another forward-looking writer like John in Revelation, this author imagines a state of perfect peace where God and God's ways rule.

But Jesus, in his preaching, also taught about a present kingdom—something discernable on earth now and not merely in some distant future. The first words the gospel of Mark places in his mouth, "The time is fulfilled, and the kingdom of God has come near; repent, and believe in the good news" (Mk. 1:15), say it directly. Further, in describing the meaning of such a thing in the parables, Jesus often compared the kingdom to seeds (see Mk. 4:26–29, 30–32), which start small but grow, or yeast (Mt. 13:33), a tiny agent that causes dough to rise and expand. The idea of a hidden treasure also appears (Mt. 13:44); it might not look so special on the surface of things, but something valuable resides beneath a rough exterior. In all these cases, what begins as inconsequential turns out to be incredibly productive, and present in the here and now. While Revelation and Isaiah depict an idealized vision of the kingdom in its final glory, Jesus encourages his followers to look for signs of it all around them today.

In that sense, the community that survives at the end of *Breaking Dawn* qualifies as an image of the kingdom. Gathered to defend the life of young Renesmee,[49] a group of vampires, shape-shifters, humans, and a human-vampire hybrid act cooperatively. Nothing like such a community could have been anticipated. Vampires, for instance, often find themselves in conflict with one another for dominance and control.[50] Vengeance frequently provides a basis for action, even between groups known for more positive relations.[51] The Quileute shape-shifters exist solely to protect the human community from vampires, which often means killing them.[52] Even though a treaty with the Cullens has kept a kind of peace,[53] and the relationship between Bella and Jacob has brought the two groups into occasional alliance,[54] a great deal of distrust and resentment remain.[55] Most humans, of course, know nothing of these groups, much less live in peace with them. Edward, for instance, tells Bella that people typically recoil from vampires in an innate defense rather than drawing close enough to develop any bonds.[56] But once Jacob shows himself phased to Charlie[57] and then brings him to meet Renesmee and see Bella,[58] Charlie shows a different possibility when he learns how to become a part of Bella's life along with some humans from the Quileute.[59] Finally, no one even knew someone like Nahuel existed,[60] and he has lived a rather forlorn existence away from any other group outside of his own family.

This child Renesmee, however, draws them all together in friendship and even love. What stands out in Meyer's story comes in the reactions Renesmee garners from all she encounters. She puts herself into people's heads with a touch and shows them her truth.[61] Without artifice and without boundaries, she opens herself to all she encounters. This ability resembles that of Jesus in the gospels to challenge human prejudice with his willingness to engage all who approach him, including tax collectors and sinners (Mk. 2:15–17), prostitutes (Lk. 7:36–50), and lepers (Mk. 1:40–41). He forges a community of followers notably different from others in that time. Indeed, one of the central attributes of the Christian church becomes its lack of barriers. According to Paul, for those persons who belong to Christ, "There is no longer Jew or Greek, there is no longer slave or free, there is no longer male or female; for you are all one in Christ Jesus" (Gal. 3:28). This new kind of kingdom allows for diverse and even hostile groups to forge a common bond and live not merely in the absence of tension, but with true respect and love for one another.

## Conclusions

The Cullen family, in its practice of respect for human life, becomes an embodiment of good in Meyer's novels. Willing denial of their nature forms them into a family capable of bonding in ways previously unknown and untried in the vampire community. That practice, further, makes it possible for Edward and the others to love Bella in her humanity and to embrace Renesmee—half-human and half-vampire—as their own. They also, as a result of their acceptance of Bella, build a relationship with the Quileute based on more than treaty obligation.

By contrast, the Volturi, supposed keepers of the peace and dispensers of justice in the vampire world, appear as a source of evil in Meyer's books. Their hunger for power and desire to sustain their position drives them to forfeit any sense of right and wrong, and they threaten the existence of the Cullens. The final confrontation assumes the air of a classic ultimate battle and, quite contrary to expectations, the Cullens emerge as victorious. Capable of gathering a diverse community bound by love and a commitment to the young Renesmee, the Cullens reflect a Christian ideal. Their victory mirrors the ultimate triumph of the church in the book of Revelation. A vastly inferior group committed to nonviolence as far as possible takes on the most powerful force known and wins via the power of truth. Although not a permanent victory—at least like the one narrated at the close of the Christian canon—the Cullens nonetheless experience the possibility of living undisturbed according to their own moral and ethical norms.

## QUESTIONS TO CONSIDER

1. The Volturi clearly, at least at some points in their history, act in ways that uphold order and preserve peace. Why, then, do they assume such a threatening presence to the Cullens? Does their presentation indicate that what one labels good or evil depends, in large measure, on circumstance rather than on some fundamental sense of identity?

2. How does the community that the Cullens create reflect the ideal of the church? Where do they vary from that image?

3. Armageddon, in cultural speech, refers to a final and decisive battle. How does the confrontation between the Cullens and the Volturi appear as such? How does it differ? Does Armageddon necessarily mean the complete and total annihilation of one side?

4. In the book of Revelation, as in most apocalyptic literature, God's ultimate victory never truly is in question. The opposing forces, although capable of great destruction, cannot stand up against the power of God. Is the defeat of the Volturi also inevitable in *Breaking Dawn*? Or do the Cullens stand a chance of losing?

# 7

# Final Thoughts

On the surface, nothing about the *Twilight* saga explicitly expresses a religious agenda. To millions of readers the romance of Bella and Edward draws in an audience entranced by the passion of forbidden and impossible love fighting for its survival. But Meyer consciously frames each of her novels with an opening quotation that shapes her writing and the reading experience. Further, in the arc of the four-book story line, the quotations suggest a Christian themed progression.

As noted previously, *Twilight* opens with Genesis 2:17 and thus not only introduces the idea of the garden of Eden and humanity's "fall" as understood in the Christian tradition, but also all of the common cultural appropriations of such. Indeed, one look at the cover reveals how the image of the fruit offered communicates the content of the story. *New Moon* takes a decidedly different approach. It builds around a quotation from Act II, Scene IV of Shakespeare's *Romeo and Juliet*:

> These violent delights have violent ends
> And in their triumph die, like fire and powder,
> Which, as they kiss, consume.

Meyer writes here about the dangers and the heartache of an all-consuming passion. This narrative pushes the idea that neither Bella nor Edward can exist apart from the other, thus giving Meyer the license to think about issues such as what death might mean to the undead, the relationship of death to any possible eternity or God, and why Edward places such a premium on Bella's humanity. Building on the first book, it functions almost as a message of "be careful for what you wish." In reaching for the forbidden fruit, Bella knows great joy, but also suffers enormous pain.

Although the actual story of *Eclipse* makes explicit references to Emily Brontë's *Wuthering Heights* in the story itself, the novel begins with Robert Frost's short poem *Fire and Ice.*

> Some say the world will end in fire,
> Some say in ice.
> From what I've tasted of desire
> I hold with those who favor fire.
> But if I had to perish twice,
> I think I know enough of hate
> To say that for destruction ice
> Is also great
> And would suffice.

Frost created a poem based on Dante's *Inferno* where the upper reaches of hell find persons struggling with desire, but the lowest depths—the icy ones—offer a home to betrayers. For Frost, and Meyer, desire is equated with fire and hate with ice. Each holds the potential to unleash enormous destructive power. But in *Eclipse*, the themes of vengeance and hate get the most play. Bella's choice for Edward causes complications between the Cullens and others in the vampire world, expressed most fully in the character of Victoria, who seeks justice for the loss of her mate, James. Additionally, the continued complications of desire as seen in the triangle of Bella, Edward, and Jacob, demonstrate its power to inflict deep and lasting pain on all involved.

Finally, in *Breaking Dawn*, Meyer introduces her story with the opening verses of Edna St. Vincent Millay's poem *Childhood is the Kingdom Where Nobody Dies.* This poem meditates on death and loss, but Meyer does not include the sad ending, as it belies the more optimistic conclusion of her novel. Instead of the poem's world, where one must grow up and suffer irreplaceable losses, Bella and her family get to exist in an eternal childhood where no one dies—the vampire version of a happily ever after. The decision Bella makes in *Twilight* for Edward—for belief in the impossible, for faith in the unseen—carries her through to an improbable conclusion. Edna St. Vincent Millay plays in her poem on the words of the apostle Paul in 1 Corinthians 13:11 about growing up and putting away childish things. There, Paul argues that humans cannot know or understand God's world in any kind of complete way because human knowledge, like the thinking of children, remains limited. But just as children grow up and mature, one day Christians will experience the fullness of God's work. Millay, however, does not buy it. In her world, childhood means an innocence that does not experience the profound hurts that batter adults, who can never understand the power of death until they experience it up close. Meyer, however, wants to go more with Paul. By the conclusion of her story, Bella knows immortality, her child is safe, her family is whole, and her love for Edward will endure forever. Just as the Christian gospel provides a way out from the choices made in Eden, so also does Bella find a way to overcome all obstacles and demonstrate the wisdom of her initial choice.

In some sense, then, the *Twilight* saga functions as the story of the spiritual journey of Bella Swan. What begins for her in a move from Arizona to Washington, from mother to father, from relatively normal to the highly extraordinary, proceeds through significant excitement, powerful loss, incredible danger, and eventually enormous gain. Similarly, Matthew 10:37–39 speaks directly of the life a follower of Jesus will lead. One must be willing to leave father and mother, son and daughter, and love Christ more. One must be willing to die. Bella, indeed, demonstrates her readiness to forge a new family and to sacrifice her life. In turn, she receives what Meyer depicts as a far greater reward. From that perspective alone, Bella emerges as an exemplar of Christian values, even in the guise of a vampire.

It would take another book to develop the idea of these books as a spiritual journey, but this end merely points readers to the myriad possibilities for reading religious themes and images in the book and will, it is hoped, prod consideration and discussion of where fiction and religion cross.

## QUESTIONS TO CONSIDER

1. Do you see Meyer as intentionally playing on the Christian story in the development of the Twilight saga, or does the pattern emerge only in the eyes of a reader seeking it out?
2. Would you consider Bella as a model for a life of faith? What qualities might commend her? What does she lack in this regard?

3. What other religious themes and images do you observe in the *Twilight* saga? Be prepared to point them out with specific references to how they emerge in the novels.

# Notes

## Chapter 1: Edward

[1]Anton Karl Kozlovic, "The Structural Characteristics of the Cinematic Christ-Figure," *Journal of Religion and Popular Culture*, 8 (Fall 2004): online.

[2]From Minucius Felix, *Octavius*, trans. R. E. Wallis, vol. 4 in The Ante-Nicene Fathers (Buffalo, N. Y.: The Christian Literature Publishing Co., 1887), 177–78.

[3]Stephenie Meyer, *New Moon* (New York: Little, Brown and Company, 2006), 482–84.

[4]Stephenie Meyer, *Twilight* (New York: Little, Brown and Company, 2005), 263–65.

[5]Ibid., 188.

[6]Meyer, *Midnight Sun*, http://www.stepheniemeyer.com/pdf/midnightsun_partial_draft4.pdf, 263.

[7]Meyer, *Twilight*, 307.

[8]Ibid., 339.

[9]Meyer, *Twilight*, 288–289.

[10]Meyer, *New Moon*, 36–37.

[11]Kozlovic, "Structural Characteristics," [5].

[12]Ibid., 18.

[13]One might think here of Sister Helen Prejean in *Dead Man Walking* , Babette in *Babette's Feast*, Superman in *Superman: The Movie,* or John Coffey in *The Green Mile.*

[14]Here, characters like Bess in *Breaking the Waves* or Luke in *Cool Hand Luke* or Sgt. Elias in *Platoon* come to mind.

[15]Kozlovic, "Structural Characteristics," [21].

[16]Meyer, *Twilight*, 79.

[17]Ibid., 135.

[18]For example, see ibid., 411–14; Stephenie Meyer, *Eclipse* (New York: Little, Brown and Company, 2007), 25–26; or Stephenie Meyer, *Breaking Dawn* (New York: Little, Brown and Company, 2008), 485.

[19]Kozlovic, "Structural Characteristics," [21].

[20]Meyer, *Twilight*, 414.

[21]Stephenie Meyer, *Breaking Dawn* (New York: Little, Brown and Company, 2008), 375–86.

[22]Kozlovic, "Structural Characteristics," [46].

[23]Meyer, *Breaking Dawn*, 387–89.

[24]Ibid., 403.

[25]Ibid., 405.

[26]Ibid., 434.

[27]Kozlovic, "Structural Characteristics," [27].

[28]See, for one example, Meyer, *New Moon*, 360–61.

[29]Meyer, *Twilight*, 210.

[30]Ibid., 56–57.

[31]Ibid., 158–62.

[32]Ibid., 166.

[33]Ibid., 472.

34Kozlovic, "Structural Characteristics," [51].

35Meyer, *Twilight*, 65.

36Stephenie Meyer, *Midnight Sun: Edward's Version of Twilight*, (unfinished draft available online at http://www.stepheniemeyer.com/midnightsun.html), 86.

37Meyer, *Twilight*, 85.

38Ibid., 211.

39Ibid., 472.

40Meyer, *New Moon*, 69–70.

41Ibid., 507–10.

42Stephenie Meyer, *Eclipse* (New York: Little, Brown and Company, 2007): 273.

43See for example, Meyer, *Twilight*, 273–74; Meyer, *Midnight Sun*, 86–87; Meyer, *Twilight*, 378–79.

44Kozlovic, "Structural Characteristics," [30].

45Meyer, *Twilight*, 19; 69.

46Ibid., 320–21.

47Ibid., 22.

48Kozlovic, "Structural Characteristics," [33].

49Ibid., [35].

50Meyer, *Twilight*, 36.

51Ibid., 19, 206.

52Ibid., 186. and Meyer, *Breaking Dawn*, 485.

53Meyer, *Twilight*, 19.

54Kozlovic, "Structural Characteristics," [65].

55Ibid.

56Meyer, *Twilight*, 24.

57Ibid., 46.

58Ibid., 229–30.

59Ibid., 376

60Kozlovic, "Structural Characteristics," [37].

61See, for example, Meyer, *Midnight Sun*, 210.

62Meyer, *Twilight*, 310.

63Kozlovic, "Structural Characteristics," [41].

64See, for example, Meyer, *Twilight*, 282.

65Meyer, *Eclipse*, 192.

66Ibid., 277.

67Meyer, *Eclipse*, 451.

68Edward enforces abstinence, at least until after the marriage ceremony in the fourth novel. The consummation of their love, however, comes not at his behest, but as a result of her demands to experience such physical love with him before she becomes a vampire and her body changes. For Edward, the primary goal of keeping Bella safe takes precedence over any sexual need he experiences, and his ability to maintain control often serves as a source of frustration in their relationship.

69Kozlovic, "Structural Characteristics," [58].

70See Mk. 5:1–13; Mt. 9:27–31; Mk. 6:37–44, for example.

71See, for instance, Mt. 9:6; Jn. 3:1–2; 5:36.

72See Mk. 8:27–9:8 (also Mt. 16:13–17:13 and Lk. 9:18–36).

73Meyer, *Twilight*, 74–75.

74Ibid., 64.

75Ibid., 89.

76Ibid., 138.

77Ibid., 92.

78Ibid., 183.

79Ibid., 183.

80Ibid., 184.
81Ibid., 196–259.
82Ibid., 260.
83Ibid., 263–78.
84Ibid., 262–63.
85Ibid., 263.
86Ibid., 278.
87Meyer, *New Moon*, 71.
88Ibid., 73–77.
89Ibid., 85–93.
90Ibid., 109–15.
91Ibid., 181–89.
92Ibid., 236–42.
93Ibid., 356–62.
94In the movie version, he also comes on the screen as a kind of apparition. This cinematic detail gives the actor, Robert Pattinson, more screen time, but does not substantially alter the experience for Bella.
95Meyer, *New Moon*, 112.
96Ibid., 116.
97Ibid., 195.
98Ibid., 527.
99Michael DeGroote, "Book Editor Points out Religious Symbolism," *Mormon Times* (April 8, 2009), http://www.mormontimes.com/people_news/newsmakers/?id=7176.
100See, for instance, Meyer, *Twilight*, 278, 304, 474.
101Ibid., 1.
102Ibid.
103Ibid., 393.
104Ibid., 430 and 432.
105Ibid., 432 and 435.
106Ibid., 497.
107Ibid., 476.
108Ibid., 475.
109Ibid., 495.

## Chapter 2: Bella

1Irenaeus, *Against Heresies*, 5.19.1, trans. Alexander Roberts and William Rambaut, in *From Ante-Nicene Fathers*, ed. Alexander Roberts, James Donaldson, and A. Cleveland Coxe (Buffalo, N.Y.: Christian Literature Publishing Co., 1885). Also revised and edited for New Advent by Kevin Knight, http://www.newadvent.org/fathers/0103.htm.
2Stephenie Meyer, *Twilight* (New York: Little, Brown and Company, 2005), 48–49.
3Ibid., 4.
4Ibid., 8.
5Ibid., 80.
6Ibid., 151.
7Ibid., 9.
8Ibid., 108.
9Ibid., 11.
10Ibid., 15.
11Ibid., 47.
12Ibid., 37.

[13]Ibid., 49.

[14]Ibid., 137.

[15]Ibid., 124.

[16]Ibid., 67,

[17]Ibid., 259.

[18]Stephenie Meyer, *New Moon* (New York: Little, Brown and Company, 2006), 234.

[19]Meyer, *Twilight*, 19.

[20]Such readings typically follow Augustine: "According to Augustine, the story of Adam and Eve presents us with the vision of a humanity lost in sin. His definition of sin focuses on the primeval act of disobedience instigated by our primeval parents." Beverly Clack, *Sex and Death* (Cambridge: Polity Press, 2002), 22.

[21]Susan Niditch, "Genesis," in *The Women's Bible Commentary (expanded edition with Apocrypha)*, ed. Carol A. Newsom and Sharon H. Ringe (Louisville: Presbyterian Publishing Corporation, 1998), 17.

[22]W. Lee Humphreys, *The Character of God in the Book of Genesis: A Narrative Appraisal*, (Louisville: Westminster John Knox Press, 2001), 37.

[23]Meyer, *Twilight*, 95.

[24]Ibid., 140. Her mother, Renee, confirms this trait in Bella with regard to the engagement. Stephenie Meyer, *Breaking Dawn* (New York: Little, Brown and Company, 2008), 18.

[25]Meyer, *Twilight*, 243.

[26]Ibid., 139.

[27]Ibid., 195.

[28]Ibid., 309–11.

[29]Stephenie Meyer, *Eclipse* (New York: Little, Brown and Company, 2007), 447–48.

[30]Meyer, *Twilight*, 413.

[31]Ibid., 473–76.

[32]Meyer, *New Moon*, 527–28.

[33]Meyer, *Twilight*, 476.

[34]Meyer, *New Moon*, 536–37.

[35]Ibid., 539–41.

[36]Laurie Sue Brockaway, *How to Seduce a Man and Keep Him Seduced* (New York: Kensington Publishing Corporation, 1998), 3.

[37]"Pink Cadillac," lyrics copyrighted by Bruce Springsteen, (ASCAP).

[38]Lisa Wilson Davison, *Preaching the Women of the Bible* (St. Louis: Chalice Press, 2006), 122.

[39]Nehama Aschkenazy, *Eve's Journey: Feminine Images in the Hebraic Literary Tradition* (Detroit: Wayne State University Press, 1995), 40.

[40]Meyer, *Twilight*, 122.

[41]Ibid., 121–26.

[42]Ibid., 184.

[43]Stephenie Meyer, *Midnight Sun: Edward's Version of Twilight*, (unfinished draft available online at http://www.stepheniemeyer.com/midnightsun.html), 9–10.

[44]Ibid., 13.

[45]See Meyer, *Twilight*, 74, 84, 88 , 173, 187, 190, 244–45 or *New Moon*, 509–12 for examples.

[46]Meyer, *Twilight*, 207.

[47]Meyer, *Midnight Sun*, 234.

[48]John Anthony Phillips, *Eve: The History of an Idea* (San Francisco: Harper & Row, 1984), 171.

[49]Meyer, *Twilight*, 278.

[50]Meyer, *New Moon*, 16.

[51]Meyer, *Eclipse*, 443.

[52]Stephenie Meyer, *Breaking Dawn* (New York: Little, Brown and Company, 2008), 25.

[53]Meyer, *Eclipse*, 446 for one instance.

[54]Meyer, *Twilight*, 365–66.

[55]Meyer, *Eclipse*, 273–74, for example.

[56]Ibid., 445.

[57]Meyer, *Midnight Sun*, 141.

[58]Meyer, *Eclipse*, 497–98.

[59]Ibid., 450.

[60]Ibid., 451—55.

[61]Ibid., 452—53.

[62]Ibid., 454.

[63]Ibid., 452–53.

[64]Meyer, *New Moon*, 71.

[65]Meyer, *Eclipse*, 31–32; 61–64.

[66]Ibid., 99–101.

[67]Ibid., 414–21.

[68]Ibid., 452.

[69]Ibid., 459.

[70]Phillips, *Eve*, 61.

[71]See Meyer, *Eclipse*, 33, 187, 443 for a few examples.

[72]Irena Makarushka, "*Women Spoken For: Images of Displaced Desire*," in *Screening the Sacred: Religion, Myth, and Ideology in Popular American Film*, ed. Joel W. Martin and Conrad E. Ostwalt, Jr. (Boulder, Colo.: Westview Press, 1995), 144.

[73]Meyer, *Eclipse*, 522–30; 594–604.

[74]Ibid., 590.

[75]Ibid., 616,

[76]Meyer, *Breaking Dawn*, 49.

[77]Richard E. Spear, *The"Divine" Guido: Religion, Sex, Money and Art in the World of Guido Reni* (New Haven: Yale University Press, 1997), 130.

[78]Meyer, *Breaking Dawn*, 24–27.

[79]Ibid., 82–83.

[80]Meyer, *Twilight*, 474; *New Moon*, 73; *Eclipse*, 333 .

[81]Meyer, *New Moon*, 511.

[82]Meyer, *Breaking Dawn*, 89.

[83]Ibid., 98.

[84]This label is not meant to downplay or minimize the horror and trauma of rape. Rather, it is a kind of cultural shorthand for talking about the sexual politics between two persons where the open expression of desire is being repressed and thus "force" becomes the avenue by which the sexual act proceeds and through which responsibility is ceded to the dominant party.

[85]Christine Seifert, "Bite Me! (Or Don't)" in *Bitch*, http://bitchmagazine.org/article/bite-me-or-dont.

[86]Jaroslav Pelikan, *Mary Through the Centuries: Her Place in the History of Culture* (New Haven: Yale University Press, 1998), 83–84.

[87]Meyer, *Breaking Dawn*, 107–8.

[88]Ibid., 126–27, 179.

[89]Ibid., 133.

[90]Ibid., 132.

[91]Ibid., 133, 179–81.

[92]Ibid., 138.

[93]Ibid., 178.

[94]Ibid., 174–77, 190–91, 233–35, 348–60, 370–75.

[95]Ibid., 399; 436–47.

[96]Ibid., 674–78.

[97]For a concise explanation of these features of Mary, see Father William G. Most, *The Blessed Virgin Mary: Her Privileges and Relation to Christ and His Church*, at http://www.ewtn.com/faith/teachings/marya1.htm.

[98]Meyer, *Breaking Dawn*, 375–403.

[99]Ibid., 426.

[100]See, for instance, the description of how she shields her family in Meyer, *Breaking Dawn*, 702.

[101]Ibid., 747

[102]Ibid., 393–95; 412.

[103]Ibid., 466.

[104]Ibid. , 182.

[105]Ibid., 428, for example.

[106]Ibid., 751.

[107]Ibid., 752.

[108]Ibid., 753–54.

## Chapter 3: Carlisle

[1]Stephenie Meyer, *New Moon* (New York: Little, Brown and Company, 2006), 36.

[2]Stephenie Meyer, *Twilight* (New York: Little, Brown and Company, 2005), 336–37.

[3]Ibid., 337–39.

[4]Meyer, *New Moon,* 36.

[5]Meyer, *Twilight*, 414.

[6]Meyer, *New Moon*, 535.

[7]Ibid., 536.

[8]Walter Brueggemann, *Genesis* (Louisville: Westminster John Knox Press, 1982), 30.

[9]Meyer, *New Moon*, 41.

[10]Stephenie Meyer, *Breaking Dawn* (New York: Little, Brown and Company, 2008), 240–41.

[11]Ibid., 376–77.

[12]Meyer, *New Moon*, 41.

[13]Stephenie Meyer, *Midnight Sun: Edward's Version of Twilight*, (unfinished draft available online at http://www.stepheniemeyer.com/midnightsun.html), 13.

[14]David B. Perrin, *Studying Christian Spirituality* (New York: Routledge, 2007), 123.

[15]Ibid., 123.

[16]See, for example, Meyer, *Twilight*, 288 or Meyer, *Midnight Sun*, 69–70.

[17]See, for example, Meyer, *Twilight*, 300–302.

[18]Meyer, *New Moon*, 428.

[19]See Meyer, *Twilight*, 125–26; *Midnight Sun*, 683; or Stephanie Meyer, *Eclipse* (New York: Little, Brown & Company, 2007), 78, for some hint of this progression.

[20]Meyer, *Breaking Dawn*, 657–61.

[21]Meyer, *New Moon*, 428.

[22]Meyer, *Twilight*, 339–41.

[23]Meyer, *New Moon*, 40.

[24]Ibid., 40.

[25]Ibid., 38–40.

[26]See Meyer, *Twilight*, 288–89 and Meyer, *Eclipse*, 159–62.

[27]Meyer, *Twilight*, 289.

[28]Ibid. and *Eclipse*, 166–67.

[29]Edward L. Greenstein, "Biblical Law" in *Back to the Sources: Reading the Classic Jewish Texts*, ed. Barry W. Holtz (New York: Simon & Schuster, 1984), 101.

[30]Rabbi Morris N. Kertzer, *What is a Jew? A Guide to the Beliefs, Traditions, and Practices That Answers Questions for both Jew and Non-Jew* (New York: Touchstone, 1996), 39.

[31]Meyer, *Twilight*, 307.

[32]Ibid., 336–37.

[33]Meyer, *Eclipse*, 167–68.

[34]Ibid., 300–301.

[35]See, for example, Jud. 2:11; 3:7; 6:1; 13:1 or Hosea 11:7 or Jer. 2:5. There are countless texts that make the point.

[36]Meyer, *Twilight*, 268–69.

[37]Meyer, *Eclipse*, 163.

[38]Meyer, *New Moon*, 28–29.

[39]See, for instance, Jud. 2:18; Hos. 11:8–9; Jer. 46:27–28.

[40]Meyer, *Midnight Sun*, 82.

[41]W.E. Nunnally, "Father," in *Eerdmans Dictionary of the Bible*, ed. David Noel Freedman, Allen C. Meyers, and Astrid Beck (Grand Rapids.: William B.Eerdmans, 2000), 457.

[42]Meyer, *Breaking Dawn*, 32.

[43]Meyer, *Twilight*, 36.

[44]Meyer, *Midnight Sun*, 80.

[45]See, for instance, ibid., 81.

[46]Meyer, *Twilight*, 377.

[47]Meyer, *Breaking Dawn*, 685–90.

[48]Meyer, *New Moon*, 334.

[49]Meyer, *Twilight*, 20–21.

[50]Meyer, *New Moon*, 82.

[51]Marianne Meye Thompson, *The Promise of the Father: Jesus and God in the New Testament* (Louisville: Westminster John Knox Press, 2000), 60.

[52]Meyer, *Twilight*, 269.

[53]Ibid., 321.

[54]Ibid., 289.

[55]See, for instance, Meyer, *Midnight Sun*, 215.

[56]Ibid., 82.

[57]Meyer, *New Moon*, 32.

[58]Meyer, *Twilight*, 341.

[59]Ibid., 343.

[60]Meyer, *Midnight Sun*, 214–15.

[61]Meyer, *Eclipse*, 569

[62]Ibid., 578–79.

[63]See Meyer, *Midnight Sun*, chapter 4.

[64]Meyer, *Eclipse*, 500–502; *Breaking Dawn*, 447–51.

[65]Meyer, *Breaking Dawn*, 549–51.

[66]Ibid., 512–17.

[67]Meyer, *Midnight Sun*, 214.

[68]Meyer, *New Moon*, 534–36.

[69]See, for example, Meyer, *Twilight*, 454–57; *New Moon*, 31–34; *Eclipse*, 567–68.

## Chapter 4: Determinism and Moral Choice

[1]David Basinger and Randall Basinger, "Introduction," in *Predestination & Free Will: Four Views of Divine Sovereignty & Human Freedom*, ed. John Feinberg, Norman Geisler, Bruce Reichenbach, Clark Pinnock (Downers Grove, Ill.: InterVarsity Press, 1986), 7.

2D. Todd Christofferson, "Moral Agency," at http://www.lds.org/ldsorg/v/index.jsp?hideNav=1&locale=0&sourceId=aed5ceb47f381210VgnVCM100000176f6 20a____&vgnextoid=2354fccf2b7db010VgnVCM1000004d82620aRCRD.

3Stephenie Meyer, *New Moon* (New York: Little, Brown and Company, 2006), 37.

4Stephenie Meyer, *Twilight* (New York: Little, Brown and Company, 2005), 308.

5Ibid., 184 and 187.

6Meyer, *New Moon*, 546.

7Meyer, *Twilight*, 304.

8See, for example, Stephenie Meyer, *Midnight Sun: Edward's Version of Twilight*, (unfinished draft available online at http://www.stepheniemeyer.com/midnightsun.html), 20.

9See, for example, Meyer, *Twilight*, 188.

10Ibid., 303.

11See, for instance, Meyer, ibid., 175, 266, and *New Moon*, 524.

12See Meyer, *Twilight*, 139.

13See, for example, ibid., 184, 190, 243.

14See Meyer, *New Moon*, 527 or Stephenie Meyer, *Eclipse* (New York: Little, Brown and Company, 2007), 600, for examples.

15The child of a broken marriage, she lived most of her life with a mother whose inability to act like an adult forced Bella into the role. (See Meyer, *Twilight*, 4.) Likewise, her father, Charlie, comes to depend on her as well. Because he cannot cook, she assumes the responsibility for shopping and meals (Meyer, *Twilight*, 31–32), and even cleans the house (Meyer, *Twilight*, 38). When Edward comes along and attends to her so closely, saves her from danger, and watches her even in her sleep, perhaps his attention and devotion meet Bella's need for security and stability. He represents the only steady thing, the only real sense of family, she has ever known.

16Meyer, *New Moon*, 508–15.

17Ibid., 84–97.

18Ibid., 529.

19Ibid., 610.

20Meyer, *Eclipse*, 111.

21Meyer, *New Moon*, 266 and 287.

22Meyer, *Eclipse*, 111–12.

23Ibid., 77.

24Meyer, *New Moon*, 272, 288, 311–12, 345, 347–48, 387.

25Meyer, *Eclipse*, 333 and 529.

26Ibid., 111.

27Meyer, *New Moon*, 309.

28Ibid., 319 and Stephenie Meyer, *Breaking Dawn* (New York: Little, Brown and Company, 2008), 205.

29Meyer, *New Moon*, 319.

30Meyer, *Breaking Dawn*, 203–5.

31Ibid., 208–12.

32Ibid., 449.

33Meyer, *Eclipse*, 123.

34Ibid., 176.

35See the Book of Moses 7:32, in *The Book of Mormon: Another Testament of Jesus Christ*, http://scriptures.lds.org/bm/contents.

36See the Book of Moses 4:1 and 3.

37See the Book of Moses 4:4.

38See the Book of Mosiah 2:41.

39Teryl Givens, *By the Hand of a Mormon: The American Scripture that Launched a New World Religion* (New York: Oxford University Press, 2002), 206.

[40]Meyer, *Twilight*, 337.
[41]Meyer, *New Moon*, 39–41.
[42]Meyer, *Twilight*, 288.
[43]Meyer, *Eclipse*, 160.
[44]Ibid., 166–67.
[45]Meyer, *Eclipse*, 292–95.
[46]Meyer, *New Moon*, 271.
[47]Meyer, *Eclispse*, 266.
[48]Meyer, *Breaking Dawn*, 126.
[49]Meyer, *Eclipse*, 167–168.
[50]Meyer, *Twilight*, 341 and *New Moon*, 38.
[51]Meyer, *Twilight*, 476 and *New Moon*, 546, for example.
[52]Meyer, *Midnight Sun*, 17.
[53]Meyer, *New Moon*, 36–37 and *Eclipse*, 273.
[54]Meyer, *New Moon*, 37 and 546.
[55]Ibid., 69.
[56]Meyer, *Eclipse*, 345.
[57]Ibid., 269.
[58]Ibid., 345.
[59]Ibid., 599.
[60]Meyer, *Breaking Dawn*, 132.
[61]Ibid., 188–92.
[62]Meyer, *Eclipse*, 521–530.
[63]Meyer, *Breaking Dawn*, 191.
[64]Meyer, *Breaking Dawn*, 354–55.
[65]Mormonism Beliefs, *Mormonism Human Nature and the Purpose of Existence*, http://www.patheos.com/Library/Mormonism/Beliefs/Human-Nature-and-the-Purpose-of-Existence.html.
[66]See, for example, Meyer, *New Moon*, 512.
[67]See Meyer, *Twilight*, 187, for Edward and Meyer, *New Moon*, 345.
[68]See, for example, Meyer, *New Moon*, 347–49.
[69]One instance can be seen in Meyer, *Eclipse*, 405.
[70]Meyer, *New Moon*, 120.
[71]One interesting portion of the story (Meyer, *Eclipse*, 528–29) deals with the complexity of their relationship and the emotional bond.
[72]See, for example, Meyer, *Eclipse*, 409 or *Breaking Dawn*, 607 or 660.
[73]Meyer, *Breaking Dawn*, 209–12.
[74]For example, see the scene in Meyer, *Eclipse*, 495–505.
[75]One example comes in Meyer, *Breaking Dawn*, 433–37.
[76]Meyer, *Eclipse*, 598.
[77]Ibid., 224.
[78]Ibid., 99–100.
[79]Ibid., 170–71.
[80]Ibid., 236–238.
[81]See, for instance, ibid., 330 or 599.
[82]Meyer, *Twilight*, 307.
[83]Meyer, *Midnight Sun*, 10–16.
[84]Ibid., 20.
[85]Ibid., 23.
[86]Meyer, *New Moon*, 509–10.
[87]See, for example, Meyer, *New Moon*, 512–13 or *Eclipse*, 500–502.
[88]Meyer, *New Moon*, 540–42.
[89]Meyer, *Eclipse*, 446–51.
[90]Meyer, *Breaking Dawn*, 133–34, 138 and 178.
[91]Meyer, *Eclipse*, 83–84.
[92]Ibid., 601–2.

[93]Meyer, *Breaking Dawn*, 577.

[94]Ibid., 615–23.

## Chapter 5: Renesmee

[1]Stephenie Meyer, *Breaking Dawn* (New York: Little, Brown and Company, 2008), 179.

[2]Ibid., 97.

[3]Ibid., 103–4.

[4]Ibid., 120–21.

[5]Ibid., 122–23.

[6]Ibid., 124.

[7]Ibid., 127 and 129.

[8]Ibid., 174.

[9]Ibid., 248–50.

[10]Ibid., 321,

[11]Ibid., 301–2.

[12]See, for one example, ibid., 177.

[13]Ibid., 133, 138 and 177.

[14]Ibid., 138 and 178.

[15]Ibid., 175–79.

[16]Herod was appointed king by the Roman Senate after a nomination in 40 B.C.E. by Marc Antony and the confirmation by Augustus in 31 B.C.E..

[17]"We have extraordinarily good historical records for the reign of Herod the Great. It is inconceivable that such a 'slaughter of the infants' would go unrecorded by the Jewish historian Josephus or other contemporary Roman historians." James D. Tabor, *The Jesus Dynasty: The Hidden History of Jesus, His Royal Family, and the Birth of Christianity* (New York: Simon and Schuster Paperbacks, 2006), 88.

[18]"His paranoia about the vulnerability of his position resulted over time in his ordering the murder of several family members, including his wife's seventeen-year-old brother, Herod's beloved wife herself, and her two remaining sons. While terminally ill and suffering in horrible pain with what was likely a kidney disease around 4 B.C.E., he also ordered the execution of a number of key Jewish leaders." John Baggett, *Seeing Through the Eyes of Jesus: His Revolutionary View of Reality & His Transcendent Significance for Faith* (Grand Rapids: Williams B. Eerdmans, 2008), 163.

[19]Meyer, *Breaking Dawn*, 34.

[20]Ibid., 35.

[21]Ibid., 544–47.

[22]Ibid., 548.

[23]Ibid., 549.

[24]Ibid., 550.

[25]See ibid., 445–46; 588–89 for examples.

[26]See ibid., 297–98 for instance.

[27]Ibid., 355.

[28]Ibid., 450–51.

[29]Ibid., 200–202.

[30]Ibid., 682–83.

[31]Ibid., 592–93; 608–13.

[32]Ibid., 515.

[33]Ibid., 589, 593.

[34]Although the text also records other resurrections with less of an impure motive in chapters 17 and 18.

[35]Meyer, *Breaking Dawn*, 503–4.

[36]Ibid., 463

[37]Ibid., 460–62.

38Ibid., 529.

39Ibid., 736–38.

40Ibid., 199–203.

41Ibid., 211–16, 229–32.

42Ibid., 586–87.

43Ibid., 687.

44Ibid., 713.

45Ibid., 731.

46Ibid., 735–39.

47Garry Wills, *What The Gospels Meant* (New York: Viking, 2008), 63.

## Chapter 6: Revelation, the Final Apocalypse, and the Coming of the Kingdom

1Stephenie Meyer, *Twilight* (New York: Little, Brown & Company, 2005), 339–40.

2Stephenie Meyer, *Breaking Dawn* (New York: Little, Brown & Company, 2008), 580.

3Stephenie Meyer, *New Moon* (New York: Little, Brown & Company, 2006), 19–20.

4Ibid., 428–31.

5Ibid., 475–76,

6Meyer, *Breaking Dawn*, 575–76.

7Ibid., 602–3.

8See also the *Catechism of the Catholic Church*, Part One, Section Two, Article I, Paragraph 7:II:391; http://www.scborromeo.org/ccc/p1s2c1p7.htm.

9James R. Lewis, *Satanism Today: An Encyclopedia of Religion, Folklore, and Popular Culture* (Santa Barbara: ABC-CLIO, Inc., 2001), 154.

10Meyer, *New Moon*, 467.

11The basic idea here becomes that the physical appearance reflects the character of any being. Thus the beauty of the angel, now fallen, transforms into something quite grotesque.

12Meyer, *New Moon*, 474–75.

13Ibid., 477–79.

14Meyer, *Breaking Dawn,*

15Merrill C. Tenney, *The World of the New Testament* (Grand Rapids: William B. Eerdmans, 1985), 14.

16Bart D. Ehrman, *The New Testament: A Historical Introduction to the Early Christian Writings*, 3d ed. (New York: Oxford University Press, 2004), 469–70.

17The argument here is an extended one. See Jon D. Levenson, *Creation and the Persistence of Evil: The Jewish Drama of Divine Omnipotence* (New York: Harper & Row, 1988).

18Meyer, *Breaking Dawn*, 679.

19Ibid., 680–83.

20Meyer, *New Moon*, 429.

21Meyer, *Breaking Dawn*, 549, 561, 574, for instance.

22Ibid., 681.

23Ibid., 692.

24Meyer, *New Moon*, 482–84.

25Meyer, *Eclipse*, 578–79.

26Meyer, *Breaking Dawn*, 707–8.

27Warren Carter notes that readers of Revelation should "locate the crisis, at least in part, in the sociopolitical pressure placed on Christians by the imperial cult, especially popular in Asia Minor as a means of uniting people and emperor. Warren Carter, "Vulnerable Power: The Roman Empire Challenged By The Early

Christians," in *Handbook of Early Christianity: Social Science Approaches*, ed. Anthony J. Blasi, Jean Duhaime, and Paul-André Turcotte (Walnut Creek, Calif.: AltaMira Press, 2002), 484.

[28]Richard A. Horsley, "Renewal Movements and Resistance to Empire in Ancient Judea" in *The Postcolonial Bible Reader*, ed. R. S. Sugirtharajah (Oxford: Blackwell, 2006), 70.

[29]Meyer, *Breaking Dawn*, 603–5.

[30]Ibid., 658.

[31]Ibid., 602.

[32]Ibid., 603.

[33]Ibid., 560–61, 570, 574–75 offer a few of the many examples.

[34]"Reagan Believed 'Armageddon was Near,'" *ABC Newsline* (http://www.abc.net.au/news/newsitems/200705/s1912095.htm).

[35]Howard Kurtz, "'Armageddon' Plan Was Put Into Action in 9/11, Clarke Says." *Washington Post*, April 7, 2004, A29, http://www.washingtonpost.com/ac2/wp-dyn/A55877-2004Apr6.

[36]See, for instance, the 1998 movie *Armageddon* starring Bruce Willis, Billy Bob Thornton, Ben Affleck, and Liv Tyler or the video game *Mortal Kombat: Armegddon* (2006). The song *Armageddon It* by Def Leppard also comes to mind immediately, as does the posthumously published series of Kurt Vonnegut writings on war published under the title *Armageddon in Retrospect*. The list, of course, could be much longer.

[37]Meyer, *Breaking Dawn*, 549–51, 558–68.

[38]Ibid., 617–25, for example.

[39]Ibid., 681.

[40]Ibid., 744.

[41]Ibid., 684.

[42]Ibid., 739–40.

[43]Carter, "Vulnerable Power," 454–55.

[44]Meyer, *Breaking Dawn*, 591–92, for example.

[45]Ibid., 697–98.

[46]Ibid., 725–40.

[47]Ibid., 717–18.

[48]Ibid., 743.

[49]Ibid., 593.

[50]Stephenie Meyer, *Eclipse* (New York: Little, Brown and Company, 2007), 288.

[51]Ibid., 306–8.

[52]Meyer, *Twilight*, 125 and Stephenie Meyer, *New Moon*, 309, for example.

[53]Meyer, *New Moon*, 558 offers one instance of such.

[54]Meyer, *Eclipse*, 381.

[55]Ibid., 392–401, demonstrates the tense atmosphere.

[56]Meyer, *Twilight*, 275.

[57]Meyer, *Breaking Dawn*, 495.

[58]Ibid., 506–7.

[59]Ibid., 516–17, depicts their initial meeting after Bella becomes a vampire. They subsequently spend other time together: 629–630 and 653, for instance.

[60]Ibid., 746.

[61]Ibid., 664.

# Bibliography

*ABC Newsline.* "Reagan Believed 'Armageddon was Near.'" http://www.abc.net.au/news/newsitems/200705/s1912095.htm.

Aschkenazy, Nehama. *Eve's Journey: Feminine Images in the Hebraic Literary Tradition.* Detroit: Wayne State University Press, 1995.

Baggett, John. *Seeing Through the Eyes of Jesus: His Revolutionary View of Reality & His Transcendent Significance for Faith.* Grand Rapids, Michigan: Williams B. Eerdmans, 2008.

Basinger, David, and Randall Basinger. "Introduction." In *Predestination & Free Will: Four Views of Divine Sovereignty & Human Freedom,* edited by John Feinberg, Norman Geisler, Bruce Reichenbach, Clark Pinnock, 7–16. Downers Grove, Illinois: InterVarsity Press, 1986.

*The Book of Mormon: Another Testament of Jesus Christ,* http://scriptures.lds.org/bm/contents.

Brockaway, Laurie Sue. *How to Seduce a Man and Keep Him Seduced,* New York: Kensington Publishing Corporation, 1998.

Brueggemann, Walter. *Genesis.* Louisville: Westminster John Knox Press, 1982.

Carter, Warren. "Vulnerable Power: The Roman Empire Challenged by the Early Christians." In *Handbook of Early Christianity: Social Science Approaches,* edited by Anthony J. Blasi, Jean Duhaime, and Paul-André Turcotte, 453–89. Walnut Creek, California: AltaMira Press, 2002.

Catechism of the Catholic Church, Second Edition. Part One, Section Two, http://www.scborromeo.org/ccc/p1s2c1p7.htm.

Christofferson, D. Todd, "Moral Agency." http://www.lds.org/ldsorg/v/index.jsp?hideNav=1&locale=0&sourceId=aed5ceb47f381210VgnVCM100000176f620a____&vgnextoid=2354fccf2b7db010VgnVCM1000004d82620aRCRD.

Clack, Beverly. *Sex and Death.* Cambridge: Polity Press, 2002.

Davison, Lisa Wilson. *Preaching the Women of the Bible.* St. Louis: Chalice Press, 2006.

DeGroote, Michael. "Book Editor Points out Religious Symbolism." *Mormon Times* (April 8, 2009), http://www.mormontimes. com/people_news/newsmakers/?id=7176.

Ehrman, Bart D. *The New Testament: A Historical Introduction to the Early Christian Writings.* Third Edition. New York: Oxford University Press, 2004.

Givens, Teryl. *By the Hand of a Mormon: The American Scripture That Launched a New World Religion.* New York: Oxford University Press, 2002.

Greenstein, Edward L. "Biblical Law." In *Back to the Sources: Reading the Classic Jewish Texts,* edited by Barry W. Holtz, 83–104. New York: Simon & Schuster Paperbacks, 1984.

Hart, Craig H. "Speeches: Our Divine Nature and Life Decisions." www.byub.org/talks/Download.aspx?id=59&md=pdf.

Horsley, Richard A. "Renewal Movements and Resistance to Empire in Ancient Judea." In *The Postcolonial Bible Reader,* edited by R. S. Sugirtharajah, 69–77. Oxford: Blackwell Publishing Ltd., 2006.

Humphreys, W. Lee. *The Character of God in the Book of Genesis: A Narrative Appraisal.* Louisville: Westminster John Knox Press, 2001.

Irenaeus, *Against Heresies,* http://www.newadvent.org/fathers/0103. htm. Translated by Alexander Roberts and William Rambaut. From *Ante-Nicene Fathers,* Vol. 1. Edited by Alexander Roberts, James Donaldson, and A. Cleveland Coxe. (Buffalo, N.Y.: Christian Literature Publishing Co., 1885.) Revised and edited for New Advent by Kevin Knight.

Kertzer, Rabbi Morris N. *What is a Jew? A Guide to the Beliefs, Traditions, and Practices That Answers Questions for both Jew and Non-Jew.* New York: Touchstone, 1996.

Kozlovic, Anton Karl, "The Structural Characteristics of the Cinematic Christ-Figure." *Journal of Religion and Popular Culture,* Vol. 8 (Fall 04): online.

Kurtz, Howard. "'Armageddon' Plan Was Put Into Action in 9/11, Clarke Says." *Washington Post,* April 7, 2004, Page A29, http:// www.washingtonpost.com/ac2/wp-dyn/A55877-2004Apr6.

Levenson, Jon D. *Creation and the Persistence of Evil: The Jewish Drama of Divine Omnipotence.* New York: Harper & Row, 1988.

Lewis, James R. *Satanism Today: An Encyclopedia of Religion, Folklore, and Popular Culture.* Santa Barbara: ABC-CLIO, Inc., 2001.

Makarushka, Irina, "Women Spoken For: Images of Displaced Desire." In *Screening the Sacred: Religion, Myth, and Ideology in Popular American Film*, edited by Joel W. Martin and Conrad E. Ostwalt, Jr., 142–51. Boulder, Colorado: Westview Press, 1995.

Meyer, Stephenie, *Breaking Dawn*. New York: Little, Brown, and Company, 2008.

_____. *Eclipse*. New York: Little, Brown, and Company, 2007.

_____. *Midnight Sun*, http://www.stepheniemeyer.com/pdf/midnightsun_partial_draft4.pdf, 2008.

_____. *New Moon*. New York: Little, Brown, and Company, 2006.

_____. *Twilight*. New York: Little, Brown, and Company, 2005.

Minucius Felix, "Octavius," translated by R. E. Wallis. In *The Ante-Nicene Fathers*, vol. 4, 177–78. Buffalo, N. Y.: The Christian Literature Publishing Co., 1887.

Mormonism Beliefs, *Mormonism Human Nature and the Purpose of Existence*, http://www.patheos.com/Library/Mormonism/Beliefs /Human-Nature-and-the-Purpose-of-Existence.html.

Most, Father William G., *The Blessed Virgin Mary: Her Privileges and Relation to Christ and His Church*, http://www.ewtn.com/faith/teachings/marya1.htm.

Niditch, Susan. "Genesis." In *The Women's Bible Commentary (expanded edition with Apocrypha)*, edited by Carol A. Newsom and Sharon H. Ringe, 13–29. Louisville: Presbyterian Publishing Corporation, 1998.

Nunnally, W. E. "Father." In *Eerdmans Dictionary of the Bible*, edited by David Noel Freedman, Allen C. Meyers and Astrid Beck, 456–57. Grand Rapids, Michigan: William B. Eerdmans, 2000.

Pelikan, Jaroslav. *Mary Through the Centuries: Her Place in the History of Culture*. New Haven: Yale University Press, 1998.

Perrin, David B. *Studying Christian Spirituality*. New York: Routledge, 2007.

Phillips, John Anthony. *Eve: The History of an Idea*. San Francisco: Harper & Row, 1984.

Seifert, Christine. "Bite Me! (Or Don't)" in *Bitch*, http://bitchmagazine.org/article/bite-me-or-dont.

Spear, Richard E. *The "Divine" Guido: Religion, Sex, Money and Art in the World of Guido Reni*. New Haven: Yale University Press, 1997.

Tabor, James D. *The Jesus Dynasty: The Hidden History of Jesus, His Royal Family, and the Birth of Christianity.* New York: Simon and Schuster Paperbacks, 2006.

Tenney, Merrill C. *The World of the New Testament.* Grand Rapids, Michigan: William B. Eerdmans, 1985.

Thompson, Marianne Meye. *The Promise of the Father: Jesus and God in the New Testament.* Louisville: Westminster John Knox Press, 2000.

Wills, Garry. *What The Gospels Meant.* New York: Viking, 2008.

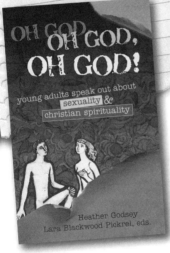